THE SHOOTING SCRIPT™

U-TURN

SCREENPLAY AND FOREWORD BY
JOHN RIDLEY

INTRODUCTION BY
OLIVER STONE

A Newmarket Shooting Script™ Series Book

NEWMARKET PRESS • NEW YORK

First Edition

10 9 8 7 6 5 4 3 2 1

Library of Congress Cataloging-in-Publication Data
Ridley, John, 1965-
U-turn : the shooting script / screenplay by John Ridley ;
introduction by Oliver Stone.
p.   c.m. — (Newmarket shooting script series)
Adaptation of the author's book, Stray dogs.
ISBN 1-55704-327-2 (pbk.)
I. Ridley, John, 1965- Stray dogs. II. U-turn (Motion picture :
1997) III. Title. IV. Series: Newmarket shooting script series book.
PN1997.U15 1997
791.43'72—dc21   97-29130
                                              CIP

Quantity Purchases

Companies, professional groups, clubs, and other organizations may qualify for special terms when ordering quantities
of this title. For information: write to Special Sales, Newmarket Press, 18 East 48th Street, New York, NY 10017;
call (212) 832-3575; or FAX (212) 832-3629.

Book design by Tania Garcia
Manufactured in the United States of America

OTHER NEWMARKET SHOOTING SCRIPTS™ INCLUDE:

Swept from the Sea: The Shooting Script
Ice Storm: The Shooting Script
Dead Man Walking: The Shooting Script
The Birdcage: The Shooting Script

The Shawshank Redemption: The Shooting Script
The People vs. Larry Flynt: The Shooting Script
A Midwinter's Tale: The Shooting Script
The Age of Innocence: The Shooting Script

OTHER NEWMARKET MOVIEBOOKS INCLUDE

The Seven Years in Tibet Screenplay and Story Behind the Film★
Men in Black: The Script and the Story Behind the Film★
*The Age of Innocence: A Portrait of the Film Based on the Novel
   by Edith Wharton*★
The Sense and Sensibility Screenplay & Diaries★
Showgirls: Portrait of a Film
*Panther: A Pictorial History of the Black Panthers and the Story
   Behind the Film*
*Mary Shelley's Frankenstein: The Classic Tale of Terror Reborn on
   Film*★
Bram Stoker's Dracula: The Film and the Legend★

Dances with Wolves: The Illustrated Story of the Epic Film★
*Far and Away: The Illustrated Story of a Journey from Ireland to
   America in the 1890s*★
Gandhi: A Pictorial Biography
The Inner Circle: An Inside View of Soviet Life Under Stalin
City of Joy: The Illustrated Story of the Film★
Neil Simon's Lost in Yonkers: The Illustrated Screenplay of the Film★
Last Action Hero: The Official Moviebook
Rapa Nui: The Easter Island Legend on Film★
Wyatt Earp: The Film and the Filmmakers★
Wyatt Earp's West: Images and Words

★ INCLUDES SCREENPLAY

CONTENTS

ABOUT THE FILMMAKERS

OLIVER STONE has been nominated for eleven Academy Awards®, as screenwriter, producer, and director, and has won three Oscars® (for writing *Midnight Express*, and as director of *Born on the Fourth of July* and *Platoon*).

Stone has also won two Directors Guild of America Awards, for *Platoon* and *Born on the Fourth of July*, and the Writers Guild of America Award for *Midnight Express*. He has also received three Golden Globe Awards for directing and one for writing.

Stone was born in New York in 1946 of a French mother and an American father. He has been a schoolteacher, a taxi driver, and a merchant marine. He served in the U.S. Infantry in Vietnam in 1967 and 1968, was wounded twice in battle, and decorated. After returning from Vietnam he completed his undergraduate degree studies at New York University Film School.

In addition to *U-Turn*, Stone has directed *Seizure* (1974), *The Hand* (1981), *Salvador* (1986), *Platoon* (1986), *Wall Street* (1987), *Talk Radio* (1988), *Born on the Fourth of July* (1990), *The Doors* (1991), *JFK* (1991), *Heaven and Earth* (1993), *Natural Born Killers* (1994), and *Nixon* (1995). Stone wrote or co-wrote *Midnight Express, The Hand, Scarface, Platoon, Heaven and Earth, Seizure, Conan the Barbarian, Year of the Dragon, Salvador, Wall Street, Talk Radio, Born on the Fourth of July, The Doors, JFK, Natural Born Killers, Nixon*, and *Evita*.

JOHN RIDLEY (Screenwriter/Executive Producer) previously wrote and directed *Cold Around the Heart*. His previously unproduced feature film screenplay credits include *Spoils of War, Zero Tolerance, Blades, A Warrior's Song, Full Contact, The Piece*, and *The Seekers*. His novel *Stray Dogs*, upon which *U-Turn* is based, came out in 1997.

He began his career as a staff writer on the Fox Television series "Rhythm and Blues" in 1992 and subsequently wrote for such hit TV series as "Martin," "Fresh Prince of Bel Air," "Def Comedy Jam," "The John Larroquette Show," and "The Show."

FOREWORD

BY JOHN RIDLEY

The first words Ernie Pandish ever tossed at me were: "Hey, you. Got a dollar? I don't have enough for my fries."

Ernie Pandish was, is, one of the greatest writers in the history of Hollywood, though most of his contributions have gone uncredited. He told me this as I fished a buck from my pocket. As far as I was concerned he was a wigged-out bum who wanted some of what I had very little of.

Later, because I wasn't sure if Ernie really was just another nutcase who fancied himself a legend, I did some checking at the Writer's Guild. Their state-of-the-art research department scoured their data base for any references to Mr. Pandish and concluded that Ernie Pandish was, is, one of the greatest writers in the history of Hollywood, though most of his contributions have gone uncredited. *The Big Combo, The Other Side of the Street, Private Hell 36, The File on Thelma Jordan, Quick Comes the Night, Kill Baby Kill* . . . All were seasoned with his writing if not stamped with his name.

I returned to Ships on La Cienega (back when there was a Ships on La Cienega) where I had first been hit up for money by Ernie, in hopes of picking the brains of one of the greatest writers in the history of Hollywood, credited or otherwise. It took four more trips before I found him again.

Once I had, I broke things down for Ernie: told him that I was new to Los Angeles, having just moved out from Wisconsin by way of New York. I'd come to L.A. to be a stand-up comedian (Ernie wanted to know if I had ever met Mort Sahl. I had not.), but as I had only met with a moderate amount of success, I decided to give writing a shot. (Nobody else in L.A. was doing that, right?) Somehow I got up the nerve to ask Ernie if he would mind taking a look at my novel *Stray Dogs,* which became the basis for the shooting script for *U-Turn.*

Stray Dogs was the child I'd conceived, unknowingly, the night I first dug Fred MacMurray and Barbara Stanwyck locked in their final, fatal embrace near the end of the Chandler/Wilder version of *Double Indemnity.* Their passion was consummated in an exchange of kisses and bullets, and from that moment forward I was hooked on Noir like it was my hot bottle-cap habit. I wanted to create my own world where lies, deceit, and loaded guns equaled love.

Ernie agreed to read what I had, and we met again in a week's time. After he finished his plate of fries he told me he thought the book was complete amoral drek populated with characters he wouldn't cross the street to urinate on if their hair was on fire. (Ernie, of course, is crazy for that kind of stuff.)

He also had some some things to say about my dialogue, mostly that it was shit. He was, I think, just trying to keep me humble. Still, every time I listen to Ernie's dialogue polish in *Appointment With Danger* . . . Sure, compared to that my writing is shit and I'll be the first to yell it from the top of the Hollywood sign.

But other than those choice comments, Ernie liked the book, going so far as to help me smooth over some of the repartee (dig the palaver between John—Bobby in the movie—and Grace, and between Robert Mitchum and Jane Russell in the Pandish-polished *Macao*).

There was a whole lot Ernie hepped me to regarding what people commonly call Noir. Good Noir, he once preached to me, isn't about snappy dialogue, nasty chicks, and people getting dead. That's just trimming. Noir is about one of two things: alienation or obsession. Sometimes both. Each represents a vacuum in the soul, and nature abhors a vacuum. In Noir the void is filled by greed or lust, or a combination that's mixed into a lethal cocktail. *Stray Dogs* serves up plenty of that brew.

I was, of course, beyond delight that a cat of Ernie's talents would even find my work worth reading, let alone that he would groove to it. So I asked him what seemed like a logical question. "How do I get it sold?"

Ernie just about choked on his fries. "You don't," he told me, although I wouldn't swear to the exact words. "You want to try getting these goddamn kids-in-suits running the show to put their balls on the line for something that ain't some guy locked in a building killing terrorists with English accents, be my guest. I tell you: Put it away. Forget it. Save it. When it's time, they'll come to you. One day they'll come to you."

"Goddamn kids," he added to that. I was still not sure whether Ernie was a sage or just a bitter old man who'd gotten screwed by the business once too often.

Seven years on, I know for a fact that Ernie is a sage. *Stray Dogs*, the novel, is in print, and the film is in theaters. And, thankfully, the script remains surprisingly faithful to the source material, which is not always the case with a book-to-film adaptation.

Most significantly, although a few other possibilities were explored, Grace remains a Native American. Grace, an outsider in her own land caught between the lust of two Anglos, is an essential, if not *the* essential, element of the novel, and the story would have lacked considerably without it. It was certainly an element worth fighting for. Francis Ford Coppola (the other genius I've had the opportunity to work with) once schooled me on screenwriting: Once you finish a piece, it's perfect. Then your job is to keep everyone else from fucking it up.

I wasn't much involved with the actual making of the movie, my arduous duties as Executive Producer largely kept me away from the set, but considering the outstanding cast I can't imagine the film being anything but really good.

I look forward to seeing the film with Ernie, to whom I owe a great deal (if not everything). I know he'll tell me, and anyone else who will listen, exactly what he thinks of my little movie.

July 23, 1997
Los Angeles

INTRODUCTION

BY OLIVER STONE

After the challenging and complicated effort to bring the life of Richard Nixon to the screen, I wanted, in a departure from my recent work, to try a new, perhaps more accessible, genre which wouldn't carry the burden of politics or "message" that is both projected from and onto so much of my work; a film that might be watched and judged on its own merits. Also, since I share the concerns expressed by many filmgoers and movie industry observers about the corrupting influence of mega-budget filmmaking (there's now an industry median of $40 million per film), I wanted to see if a more reasonable approach could still work.

The modestly budgeted ($20 million) *U-Turn* afforded that opportunity. John Ridley's script *Stray Dogs*, based on his yet-to-be-published book of the same title, was laced with fresh dialogue and darkly humorous characters caught up in truly absurd circumstances. I was hooked by the underlying tones of greed and desperation, and by the relationship between a small-time Vegas gambler and a desolate Arizona town where nothing is as simple as it seems. Throughout the script, constructed as a thriller with its themes of jealousy, sex, money, murder, and betrayal, Ridley maintained the fundamental tension of "what happens next" while paying stylistic homage to his beloved film noir of the 1940s.

Many of us felt the script was missing some deeper and darker insights into the psyche of its characters. Film noir characters, it seems, are generically caught, trapped. There's an overriding sense of despair which comes from the disillusioned post-War period when existentialism first reared its head at the tables of French coffee houses. Every moment being potentially life-deciding, we as individuals must take responsibility for our every choice, yet on the way to the coffin, these inhabitants of the noir world all find themselves making desperate choices—right, wrong, usually wrong, their decisions generally resulting in their deaths. We as audience members empathize because, at the end of the day, we all make lousy choices. We all feel, at times, that we lead second-rate lives, that we're losers, and we know that we will all die. These are constants, the axioms of the noir world.

With one of my writing partners from *Natural Born Killers*, Richard Rutowski, who shares my love of the Southwest American desert, I began rewriting, trying to create more conflict by increasing the sexual tension between the characters. We wanted a suffocating, slow realization for our "innocent" Bobby Cooper (Sean Penn) and our audience that this was the kind of small town where sex has become a bargaining chip for survival, a power source for control, and a bond that ties the town together. We also wanted to provide a level of perversity and tragedy for our femme fatale (Jennifer Lopez), so that she would stand out from the traditional dame with the iron heart.

Bobby Cooper, for sure, is not your classic all-American boy (Sean Penn?), but he isn't a cold-blooded killer either, at least not before he arrives in Superior. But how far will he go when he's desperate? Can he save himself from the impending punishment promised by the Russian Las Vegas gangsters who want payback on his gambling debt? We wanted to weave a subtler, larger web of conspiracy around Bobby, a paranoid sense that the town of Superior itself was pulling the strings from which Bobby found himself dangling. This spider's trap includes the hick mechanic Darrell (Billy Bob Thornton), Sheriff Potter (Powers Boothe), and perhaps even the denizens of the grocery store and the coffee shop. And what about Grace? Is she using Bobby to buy her freedom and get out of town? Or does she, in the end, truly care for and love him?

We worked on something more to motivate Grace's husband, Jake (Nick Nolte), something that would make him want to kill Grace. And the same goes for Grace. What had Jake done that was so bad? These are questions Bobby will receive clues to during the course of the movie but will ignore, as, probably, will the audience. And, of course, part of the fun of making these movies lies in those questions, the answers to which will not become clear until the very last act when we find, as in a good novel, the darker motives all boil to the surface.

In devising a stylistic approach to this thriller, we found ourselves combining elements of Noir with the Western. (I've always been attracted to the mixing and updating of genre elements; we tried this in *Natural Born Killers*, combining the road movies with the prison breakout genre, interwoven with a nineties media sensibility.) The gambler; the land baron; his Indian half-breed wife; the tough, laconic sheriff; the mechanic who could be a nineteenth-century blacksmith or horse teamster—each character is born of the Western and shares the tapestry of a small desert town to which the outsider comes one day, igniting the explosion of the subconscious. Now, of course, people drive through the Southwest. They stay in motels. They buy and sell cheap land. They make deals. They hustle. They fuck. They kill. They come and they go to—I don't know where. To nowhere. There's a nothingness about the land, a feeling of emptiness. It speaks to me of America far more than any other single region of the nation, and reflects my own innermost cultural totems about this country.

Conversely, there's a religious quality to the emptiness of the desert. The rocks tell stories. The sky is old. Everything is old. It's forever, an eternity, and you could easily get lost out there, blend into the oneness. The noir elements emerge from loneliness and alienation of the landscape, with its people living on the edges of despair, their actions resulting in nihilism. Paralleling this is Superior, Arizona itself, once a booming miners' town, now fallen onto ghostly economic times, and thus part of the film's theme of downfall. It is not surprising that less than a hundred years before, the Apaches in the area had been exterminated so that profit could be extracted from the sacred mountains ringing the town. The town may have temporarily prospered from its greed, but in time, as suggested by the blind man character of Jon Voight, it paid the price of its karma.

In taking on this "neo-Western" mode, we decided to use the volatile reversal stock that I had first seen back at New York University film school in the late 1960s. It exaggerates the primary colors and lends a harsh sense of desert light—lots of glaring oranges, reds, greens, yellows. In expressionistic splashes, it burnishes the golds and the dust and the canyons and cliffs and frontal surfaces of the town to create a raw outdoor look more apropos to "film soleil" than film noir.

I very much wanted to incorporate the music of Ennio Morricone, who had become famous for his exotic Sergio Leone themes in *The Good, The*

Bad and The Ugly, Once Upon a Time in the West, For a Few Dollars More, and *Once Upon a Time in America*. Ennio is now in his late sixties, but it was one of the great pleasures of my career to work with this man so intimately. Our association culminated in a wild recording session this last summer in Rome, where I heard sounds, some of them lunatic and ridiculous, that few American composers would allow themselves to try. There were several arguments with Ennio, who comes of a stubborn stock, but from those arguments grew the beginnings of a musical style which is a strange new blend of the Western and Ennio's romantic sexual terrorist side. I suppose you might call the resulting mongrel *spaghetti noir*.

We could not use the title *Stray Dogs*, as it was too similar to that of a film by Akira Kurosawa called *Stray Dog*, which was made in 1949. Kurosawa's lawyers contested our usage, saying it was an infringement of their copyright on the name and would cause potential confusion between the two films. After losing a legal battle with the arbitration board, we had to find a new title. During the shooting of the movie, as an incentive to our cast and crew, we held a contest offering a large financial reward to the person who came up with the best new title. Many tempting and creative suggestions were given to me on napkins, call sheets, scratch paper, and computer printouts, but the concept of *U-Turn* had stayed with me from an earlier scout, for another film, in the vast Moroccan desert—a title emblematic of our lives, as we find ourselves caught at one climax or another, trying to escape from where we have come and from what we have become.

We submitted the script without cast but with a modest budget to a small group of financiers who, surprisingly, passed on it. Shortly, however, we found the right partner in Mike Medavoy, who was then starting his own company, Phoenix Pictures, in association with Sony Pictures, and had invested in a film my company had produced, *The People vs. Larry Flynt*. Mike and I had previously worked together on *The Hand* in 1981 and *Platoon* in 1986 at Orion, and also *The Doors* in 1991 at TriStar. He read the script overnight and the next morning said he would do the film at the price we suggested without any cast or other conditions. This was an act of great faith that many directors would like to see more of, given that directors often feel trapped into having to use the same stars in the same roles time and again. The irony, of course, is that in the end we were lucky enough to assemble a superb and fresh cast without having to spend much money, which thoroughly surprised me.

After having made eleven films, it might seem that putting together a film like this would be a simple process for me. But it never is. I can even say that the process has become more difficult over the years, due to the fact that far more is expected of me now than when I started out as an unknown. For one thing, I am judged more harshly because at this stage of my career I carry a profile, a stereotype, and people are reluctant to allow me to try new forms; additionally, crew and especially actors expect to be paid at the highest levels. But we decided at the outset that nobody was going to get rich off the making of this film, unless it did well at the box office, an attitude that may not have been attractive to the actors and actresses who turned it down.

Sean Penn was my first choice for the lead. We'd wanted to work together for a long time and he very much liked the script, but he could not get his schedule to work due to a prior film commitment. I then found another respected and talented actor. We began auditioning the other roles and rehearsing for the shoot. But after a few intense sessions of rehearsal, our actor had become so immersed in the character that he realized, for personal reasons, this was a very difficult, if not impossible, role for him to perform. To borrow an image from the movie, "our radiator hose blew out," and the actor called me to say that he was heartbroken, but he just could *not do* this film, which was beginning in a few days. I can tell you, there is no more sinking feeling than having an entire cast and crew assembled in a small town in the middle of the Arizona desert ready to begin and suddenly finding yourself lacking a protagonist!

Putting the best face on things, my producers and I flew back to Los Angeles and, in a frantic thirty-six-hour period, worked with Mike Medavoy to locate a replacement. As destiny would have it, Sean Penn was now available because his other film had fallen through, and after one meeting with Sean at my house on a Saturday afternoon, he said in his flat, tough-guy voice: "I'm in."

We talked about delaying the start date, but as we were looking at Christmas break on the back end whereby the cost of the film would skyrocket, we both knew we were going to roll it in a week's time, with or without rehearsal for Sean. I had the utmost confidence, however, in his ability to become "Bobby Cooper," as I felt Sean resembled our protagonist in several ways. Sean is very much the gambler in his own field. Then, on the first day of shooting, which involved Bobby arriving in town sleepless after having been on the road all night, Sean himself showed up looking like a car wreck after an all-night drive from Los Angeles. Such ironies would abound throughout the shoot.

I also had the good fortune to work with a newcomer, Jennifer Lopez, as the dark heart of the film, Grace. Jennifer's look in *Money Train* had seduced me from the beginning, but I did not know then what her performance in *Selena* would do for her career. She fit in every way our vision of a native Apache woman living in the Southwest married to an older white man, who was going to be played by Nick Nolte. Nick had committed to the film early and stayed with it through all its bumps, as we had tried for many years to work together. In an ugly buzz cut and a graying beard, Nick stretched himself to play an older man who was not particularly attractive—in fact, you might say psychotic—but he seemed eager to do so in his constant desire to expand his range.

Powers Boothe, who had seemed so effortless to me as Alexander Haig in *Nixon*, stepped into the supporting role of the sheriff, which grew in importance as the film progressed. Jon Voight also surprised us by accepting a small and difficult part as a blind Indian, which gave Jon the chance to act out some of his sympathies for the Indian cause in this country. Billy Bob Thornton *(Slingblade)* and Claire Danes *(Romeo and Juliet)* were both major coups for our small film, Billy Bob embodying the cunning and craft of the crazed car mechanic Darrell, and Claire the mentality of the moronic teenage sexpot Jenny. Both of them were about to become world famous as we were shooting and editing, but at that time were relatively unknown. (One thing I've come not to underestimate is how swiftly change occurs in the movie business.) Joaquin Phoenix as Claire's densely aggressive and equally stupid boyfriend Toby was a revelation to me in a totally different performance from his *To Die For* role, and I still laugh no matter how many times I see his performance.

In taking on Superior, our art department literally refaced much of the main street of the town to solidify its 1950s stopped-in-time look, through which our 1990s-attired ghosts could wander. We often visited the Apache Indian reservation nearby as Jennifer Lopez familiarized herself with the culture. The concept of their tribal fate naturally wove itself into our script as we perceived them both as hostages on the land and, at the same time, its true rulers and sometime predators. If the continual rape of Grace is symbolic of the miners' exploitation of the Indians, then fate comes full circle by the end of our film, with its last towering shot of Apache country, forever brooding and silent.

The shoot itself was a short but arduous one. It was supposed to be thirty-seven days but ran to forty-two (most of our schedules have run fifty to sixty-five days) when the difficulties of working in the canyons and cliffs and the rugged exteriors of wind and sun and rock took their toll. We were lucky in that it was wintertime and the heat acceptable but, by the same token, our exterior window of light was much smaller.

Our first cut of the film revealed that no matter how fast our actors spoke, it was becoming tedious to the ear to hear as much dialogue as we had written. No matter how brilliant the dialogue is, even if it is a Wilder or a Lubitsch or a Mike Nichols film, I believe that after a certain point dialogue *ceases to work*, and looks, body language, and pure cinematic action must take over. In short, the problem with the original script was that there was too little action and far too much dialogue. As a result, quite a bit of the script was either rewritten to intensify the level of action, or was cut prior to shooting, and much of what was not cut was further pared in the editing process. I think those who study film should be aware that on paper dialogue generally reads quite a bit faster than it plays on screen.

Having written or co-written many screenplays, I view the scriptwriting process as a *process*, as being part of a team, a collaboration among filmmakers. Many don't view it this way and separate the script from the organic whole. But screenplay writing is different from the novel in that it truly grows from the intelligence and instincts of many good minds. The screenplay in its first phase is, of course, the birth mother to all the endeavors of the cast and crew, but in its second phase, during production, the script is never static on one of our films; it will go through many phases of regeneration in the actors' performances, the director's interpretation, the cinematographer's light, the art director's design, the producer's framework. And in the final, third stage of this elaborate, year-long laboratory experiment, editing itself becomes another form of rewriting, where much of the original structure may well be called into question and fundamentally altered; at least, it has been on several of my films. Thus writing is not at all a dormant process but a dynamic and changing one. The script may well be the work of one man, but the collaboration of collective souls is a movie.

You will notice when you read the script that neither Rutowski's nor my name is on the title page. This is because the Writer's Guild's rule states that in order for a film director to receive writing credit, he must have contributed at least 50 percent of the script. I think our contribution was about 40 percent, but this is not something that bothers me. It's a rule intended to protect the original author, and I have been on the other side of the fence. I do feel, however, that, space permitting, the ideal film book would contrast John Ridley's script with the shooting script, so that you would further understand the stages through which a film goes. The script that follows is as close to the edited version of the film as we could get at the time of this writing, when we were still editing and making changes in *U-Turn*.

Ultimately, what we were going for—and I hope the script conveys this to you—was a blend of the light with the dark, the yin with the yang. In the course of one tight, Aristotelian, twenty-four-hour time period, our protagonist, a gambler without too many moral scruples, goes up and down in his situation like a monkey on a ladder, his luck changing from one incident to the next. He will never quite know if he's ahead or behind in the game until the very last moment. Such, I believe, is life, although I also believe that, at the end of the day, it is not chance but character that determines your destiny, and in this regard our gambler may fall short.

In any case, I hope you will be kept in suspense as to how the dice will fall in Superior, Arizona. In the same vein, I feel strongly this is not the sort of film where one talks about the middle or the end because that would give away far too much. As was the case in theaters when I grew up, I wish our exhibitors would maintain a stricter policy of not allowing audience member into a thriller after the first ten minutes and that the reviewers would not reveal what happens after Bobby's initial entry into the town.

If you are an aspiring director or film buff, there is much to be learned from reading a script and seeing the film. You certainly will have a chance to visualize how you would shoot the scenes while you're reading it, and when you finally go and see it, you will, I hope, at least understand our approach. Anyway, whatever you decide, I hope it will be a learning experience and that you enjoy our movie. And if you ever find yourself out in the desert and your car comes up limping and you see a sign that says Superior, Arizona, please take my advice, based on the experience of a young man I've come to know quite well—and make a fast U-Turn.

August 13, 1997
Los Angeles

<u>U-Turn</u>

Screenplay by
John Ridley

NOTE

This shooting script was extensively worked on by Oliver Stone and Richard Rutowski from earlier versions by John Ridley. As explained in Oliver Stone's introduction, this script is "as close to the edited version of the film as we could get at the time of this writing, when we were still editing and making changes in *U-Turn*."

1 EXT. SOMEWHERE IN THE DESERT SOUTHWEST - DAY 1

BEGIN TITLES OVER:

It is early morning and already hot. INSECTS drone, crackle, and scurry for shade. PRAIRIE DOGS burrow to escape the sun. We can see the heat shimmering off the surface of the Earth.

On a dusty highway, a pair of VULTURES dine on a dead coyote. One of them snags an intestine and tugs a few feet of it out of the carcass.

In the distance, where a long, dusty road meets the horizon, a small shape appears -- a Sixty-four-and-a-half Mustang convertible, its top down. Its candy-apple red burns like a brilliant fireball under the sun. As the car drifts closer, we see steam escaping from under the hood. Sammi Smith's "Please Help Me Get Through The Night" plays on the car's radio.

2 INT. BOBBY COOPER'S MUSTANG - DAY 2

At the wheel, ignoring impeding disaster, BOBBY COOPER, young, good-looking, fiddles with the RADIO dial, annoyed only to find country stations. He's been driving since noon yesterday and it shows -- along with a heavily-bandaged left hand resting on the steering wheel. He finds something by Pearl Jam or Smashing Pumpkins and he cranks it. He pops a Percodan with his good hand as, in the shimmering distance ahead, he sees black shapes in the road and lays on the horn.

> BOBBY
> Get off the goddamn road!

3 EXT. DESERT ROAD - DAY 3

As the MUSTANG powers by, the VULTURES move off the shoulder, silently watching.

4 INT. MUSTANG - DAY 4

The RADIO blares as BOBBY fights to stay awake. His attention is caught by blue and red lights flashing in the oncoming lane. He sits up as the POLICE CAR (SHERIFF POTTER inside) closes quickly. The SIREN starts faintly, then SCREAMS as the cruiser roars past at speed.

> BOBBY
> Fuck you!

There is a loud pop from the front of the Mustang and a thick cloud of steam now pours from the hood. The temperature gauge starts rising.

(CONTINUED)

4   CONTINUED: 4

                          BOBBY
                 No!...Not now!...Shit!

A couple of SEMIS roar past in the opposite direction,
buffetting the Mustang with their air waves.

5   EXT. FORK IN THE ROAD - DAY   5

The car rolls into a fork in the road, limping with the droop of
an animal that won't make another hundred yards.

One sign on the larger road says "GLOBE" is 29 miles away. The
other sign, on the lesser road, tells us "SUPERIOR" is only 2
miles. A third sign confirms his destiny with "Gas, Food, 1
Mile."

BOBBY seems to have no choice. He aims the car down the lesser
road towards "Superior, Arizona."

6   EXT. OUTSKIRTS SUPERIOR - DAY   6

The car rattles on its last legs, as BOBBY mutters incantations,
noticing a old, ghostlike MINING COMPANY at the base of the
mountains overlooking the TOWN. It's deserted now, no one
visible, the gates shut, but in its vast, dark bulk, we sense
the ancient richness and power of this town. Bobby moves on.

7   EXT. HARLIN'S GARAGE - DAY   7

Down the road from the MINING COMPANY, BOBBY'S CAR pulls into a
small GAS STATION, made of weather-beaten wood, its windows long
since dusted over. The pumps themselves look to have been
manufactured in the early fifties. Above the station is a sign
so faded it's barely readable: HARLIN'S.

Bobby gets out of the car and with great care, favoring his
bandaged left hand which seems to give him a great deal of pain,
he opens the hood. A plume of steam hits him in the face.

                          BOBBY
                 Oh shit!

Bobby looks around for someone, anyone. After a few moments he
reaches into the car and blows the horn. He waits, then blows
it again. From out of the station walks DARRELL - a
slow-looking man in coveralls caked with grease and dirt. He
looks the part of a yokel.

                          BOBBY
                 You Harlin?

                          DARRELL
                 Nope. Darrell.

                              BOBBY
                    Harlin around?

                              DARRELL
                    He's up at the Look Out.

Darrell points a scraggly finger at a plateau in the distance.

                              BOBBY
                    Will he be back soon?

                              DARRELL
                    Doubt it. He's dead. The Look Out's a
                    cemetery.

                              BOBBY
                    You own this place?

                              DARRELL
                    Yep.

                              BOBBY
                    Then why do you call it Harlin's?

                              DARRELL
                    'Cause Harlin used to own it.

                              BOBBY
                    But he's dead.

                              DARRELL
                    So?

Bobby is confused, but chooses to drop the matter.

                              BOBBY
                    You want to take a look at my car? I think
                    the radiator hose is--

                              DARRELL
                    Damn. Gonna be another hot one today.
                    Sometimes I don't even want to get out of
                    bed. Course don't want to get out for the
                    cold one's neither. Then of course the
                    clouds come in...

Darrell mops his brow with a greasy rag. It doesn't so much
wipe the sweat as it does streak his forehead with dirt.

                              BOBBY
                    Look, Harlin, I've got places to be.

                       DARRELL
Darrell--

                       BOBBY
OK. Darrell... Could you just take a look
at my radiator hose. It's busted

Darrell is clearly upset at being cut off. He leans into the
car and looks at the engine.

                       BOBBY
So?

                       DARRELL
It's your radiator hose. It's busted.

                       BOBBY
I know it's busted. What did I just tell
you?

                       DARRELL
Well, you know so much why don't you just
fix it yourself?

                       BOBBY
If I could do you think I'd be standing
here wasting my time. Can you fix it, or
do I have to go somewhere else?

                       DARRELL
Somewhere else? Mister, somewhere else is
fifty miles from here. Only other gas
station down in town closed 3 years ago
when the mine got shut...

                       BOBBY
Okay, I'm stuck. You happy? Now can you
fix it, or not?

                       DARRELL
Yeah, I can fix it.

                       BOBBY
Great!

                       DARRELL
Gotta run over to the yard and see if I can
find a hose like this one, or close enough.
Gonna take time.

                       BOBBY
How much time?

(CONTINUED)

                    DARRELL
          Time.

                    BOBBY (rewinds his watch)
          What time is it now?

                    DARRELL
          Twenty-after-ten.

                    BOBBY
          Jesus. Twenty-after-ten and it must be
          ninety already.

                    DARRELL
          Ninety-two. Course half hour from now
          might be seventy-two. These clouds move
          around alot.

Bobby wipes the bandaged hand across his forehead.

                    DARRELL
          What happened to your hand?

Self-consciously Bobby quickly drops his hand to his side.

                    BOBBY
          Accident.

                    DARRELL
          You got to be more careful. Hands is
          important. Let me show you something. When
          I was a kid, now I don't know if you can
          still see it, but I gashed my fingers in a
          lawnmover.

                    BOBBY
          I'm very interested in this but is there
          someplace...

                    DARRELL
          Diner up a piece. Not much, but us simple
          folk like it.

                    BOBBY
          I'll be back in a couple of hours. And be
          careful with her, will you?

Darrell slams down the hood.

                    DARRELL
          Just a car.

7   CONTINUED: (4)   7

Bobby reaches into the car, pulls out a small ugly gym bag which
he slings onto his shoulder and moves to the trunk, pops it open.

                    BOBBY
          It's not just a car. It's a sixty-four and
          half Mustang covertible. That's the
          difference between you and me, and why you
          live here and I'm just passing through.

The trunk lid rises in the air, partially blocking Bobby from
Darrell, acting as a partition between them.

                    BOBBY
          Now do you mind? I got to get some stuff
          out of the trunk.

He throws the car key to Darrell who takes the hint, spits
grotesquely into the dirt, scratches his nuts, and walks back to
the shack.

Concealed by the trunk lid, Bobby pulls out a GUN (a .9mm black
Baretta), wrapped in a t-shirt, from the top of the bag. Perhaps
we see a flash of green money, lots of it. Sports pages and
betting sheets are piled inside. With a look around, Bobby takes
the gun and stashes it underneath the rubbermat in the trunk.
Briefly we notice a towing ROPE under the mat. There is a small
travel bag, from which he peels a fresh bottle of Percodan,
quickly taking two, as well as the sports page.

8   INT. HARLIN'S GARAGE - DAY   8

DARRELL watches out of the darkened office through the front
window, as BOBBY slams the trunk and starts walking down the
road, with the bag on his shoulder.

9   EXT. DESERT ROAD - LATER   9

BOBBY walks along a dusty patch of road into town past a sign
saying "SUPERIOR - HOME OF THE GOLDEN DOOR RETIREMENT
COMMUNITY." As he walks on, a pair of MOTORCYCLERS roar past on
their Harleys blanketing him in a cloud of DUST. He shouts
after them, but his words are lost under the whine of the cycle
engines.

10   EXT. SUPERIOR MAIN STREET - DAY   10

BOBBY hits town, such as it is: The Freeway left here a few
years back. There are only a few little stores: A general
store, a catalog outlet, a post office that doubles as a bus
depot. All of them built for the desert heat. The busiest spot
in town seems to be the truckstop/diner with a few 18 wheelers
parked outside it.

                                                            (CONTINUED)

At the corner of one street sits an old BLIND MAN dressed in
raggedy clothes, perhaps an Indian. His SEEING EYE DOG lies next
to him. He's talking to TWO OLD MEN, veterans perhaps, Indian or
Spanish. They both have missing limbs and slide off with furtive
alcoholic looks as Bobby passes. The Blind Man yells out in an
American Indian accent.

                    BLIND MAN
          Hey! You there!

                    BOBBY
          You want something, old man?

                    BLIND MAN
          Don't call me old man. Ain't you got
          respect, boy?

                    BOBBY
          You want something?

                    BLIND MAN
          Yeah I want something. I want you to run
          over to that machine and get me a pop.

                    BOBBY
          You can't do that yourself?

                    BLIND MAN
          Hell no, I can't do that myself. I'm
          blind. Can't you see that?

                    BOBBY
          I'm sorry, I didn't--

                    BLIND MAN
          What'd you think I was doing out here
          with these glasses on? Sunnin' myself?

                    BOBBY
          I don't know. I thought you were keeping
          the sun out of your eyes.

                    BLIND MAN
          I ain't got no eyes. You want to see?

                    BOBBY
          Christ no!

                    BLIND MAN
          Lost my eyes in Vyee-et-nam. Lost them
          fighting the commies. Fought the war and
          lost my eyes fightin' the commies just so
                    (MORE)

                                              (CONTINUED)

10   CONTINUED: (2)   10

                        BLIND MAN (cont'd)
              you could come around here and make fun of
              me.

                        BOBBY
              I said I was sorry.

                        BLIND MAN
              Don't be sorry. Just run over there and
              get me my pop before I die of thirst.

                        BOBBY
              Yeah, sure. You got change?

                        BLIND MAN
              Change? You want my change? I fought the
              war and lost my eyes just so I could give
              you my change?

                        BOBBY
              All right, old man. Christ.

Bobby walks across the street to a very old soda machine; it has
bottles instead of cans. The blind man shouts to Bobby.

                        BLIND MAN
              Get me a Dr. Peppa! I don't want no Colas.
              Colas ain't nothing but flavored water.

                        BOBBY
              Yeah, yeah.

Bobby puts change in the machine and pulls out a bottle of Dr.
Pepper. He starts back to the blind man.

                        BLIND MAN
              Don't forget to open it for me. I can't be
              opening my own bottle.

                        BOBBY
              Christ!

Bobby goes back to the machine and opens the bottle, then walks
back to the old man who pours a splash on the ground.

                        BLIND MAN
              A little for Mother Earth. I'm about fifty
              percent Indian, you know. To all our
              relations.

He takes a hearty swig of the soda.

                        BLIND MAN
              Ah! Just what I needed. Want some?

                                              (CONTINUED)

The blind man holds the bottle out to Bobby. A string of saliva
runs from his lips to the bottle's neck.

>   BOBBY
>   I'll pass.

Bobby reaches down and pets the old man's dog. Flies buzz around
both the dog and the Blind Man.

>   BOBBY
>   I think you'd better give your pooch a sip.
>   He looks sick.

>   BLIND MAN
>   That's 'cause he's dead.

Bobby jumps back.

>   BOBBY
>   Oh, Jesus.

>   BLIND MAN
>   I hope you wasn't pettin' him none, was
>   you?

>   BOBBY
>   What the hell are you keeping a dead dog
>   around for?

>   BLIND MAN
>   He's only just dead. What was I supposed
>   to do with him? I can't take him away
>   anywhere. And nobody wants to take him for
>   me. Do you?

>   BOBBY
>   Hell no!

>   BLIND MAN
>   See. Ain't nothing I can do but keep him
>   here beside me. That's where he belongs
>   anyways. Me and Jesse, that's my dog, not
>   anymore, but me and Jesse we been pals
>   since the war when I lost my eyes. He was
>   just a pup then... a companion that's
>   loyal, that'll keep coming back to you no
>   matter how much you kick him...I miss him.
>   (as Bobby moves away) I'll see ya later,
>   unless I come across something worse.

Bobby noticing a beautiful woman down the street, GRACE McKENNA,
compulsively turns and catches up to her. She is dressed better
than the normal t-shirts and tank tops of this town -- perhaps a

mail-ordered dress or a mother's hand-me-down. With her raven
hair and caramel skin, it is obvious she is Native American. Her
arms are full with an awkward package she can barely manage.

                    BOBBY
          Can I give you a hand, beautiful?

                    GRACE
          I'm just going to my car.

                    BOBBY
          That's right on my way.

                    GRACE
          My mother told me never to accept offers
          from strangers.

                    BOBBY
          My name is Bobby. Now I'm not a stranger
          anymore. See how easy it is for us to get
          to know each other, beautiful?

                    GRACE
          Do you have to call me that?

                    BOBBY
          I don't know your real name.

                    GRACE
          Maybe I don't want you to.

Grace stops walking.

                    BOBBY
          Maybe, but if you didn't I think you would
          have kept on walking.

                    GRACE
          You're pretty full of yourself, aren't you?

                    BOBBY
          I like that about me, beautiful.

                    GRACE
          It's Grace.

                    BOBBY
          May I carry your package, Grace?

Grace hesitates, then gives the package to Bobby. He has
trouble with it himself.

                    BOBBY
          Jesus.

                                              (CONTINUED)

                         GRACE
          You sure you can manage?

                         BOBBY
          I got it.

                         GRACE
          Do you want me to carry your pack for you?

Bobby blurts out emphatically:

                         BOBBY
          No!

He catches himself, and softens a bit.

                         BOBBY
          No, I've got it.

                         GRACE
          What happened to your hand?

                         BOBBY
          Accident.

                         GRACE
          You should be more careful.

They start walking towards Grace's car.

                         GRACE
          It's very nice of you to help me. That
          package is kind of heavy, and it's so hot.

                         BOBBY
          No trouble at all, really.

They get to a car and Bobby puts down the package.

                         BOBBY
          Wasn't nothing.

                         GRACE
          Oh, this isn't my car. It's down a ways.
          I should have parked closer. I just didn't
          think it would be so heavy. I could drive
          up.

                         BOBBY
          That's all right. I got it.

Bobby takes up the package and they begin walking again. The
package seems to have gained weight.

                                                   (CONTINUED)

                    GRACE
          It's just new drapes and curtain rods. If
          I had known it was going to be so heavy I
          would have had them delivered up to the
          house.

Bobby struggles with the package. Sweat starts to sheet his
face.

                    BOBBY (panting)
          That a fact?

                    GRACE
          I just got tired of looking at the old
          drapes. My mother made them. Had them long
          as I can remember. You ever seen something
          and just knew you had to have it?

                    BOBBY (straining)
          Yes, I have.

                    GRACE
          'Course they cost a little more than I
          should really be spending. But, damn it, I
          don't hardly ever do anything nice for
          myself. I deserve nice things.

                    BOBBY (can barely talk)
          I . . . can't . . . argue . . .

They arrive at a JEEP SAHARA.

                    GRACE
          This is it.

Bobby practically drops the package. He is covered with sweat.

                    GRACE
          Thank you, Bobby.

                    BOBBY
          You're welcome, Grace.

                    GRACE
          You're not from around here, are you?

                    BOBBY
          Why you say that? Just because I help a
          lady with her package?

                         GRACE
          You don't have that dead look in your eyes
          like the only thing you live for is to get
          through the day.

                         BOBBY
          I just drove in this morning.

                         GRACE
          Drove into Superior? What for?

                         BOBBY
          Didn't have a choice. My car overheated up
          the road.

                         GRACE
          You're lucky you didn't break down in the
          desert. Day like today, you'd be dead in no
          time. When you leaving?

                         BOBBY
          Not until my car's fixed. I don't know how
          long that's going to take.

                         GRACE
          And here I've made you all hot and sweaty.

Grace steps to Bobby and places her hand against his chest. She
rubs away some of the sweat. They look at each other a beat. A
POLICE CAR, seen earlier, pulls up beside them from behind and
idles. SHERIFF VIRGIL POTTER is a weathered, handsome,
middle-aged man with suspicious eyes, black haired in contrast
to Bobby's sandiness.

                         SHERIFF
          Morning Grace.

                         GRACE
          Morning Sheriff. Got my drapes.

                         SHERIFF
          Well it's about time. Looks like you found
          yourself a helper too.

Bobby wants to shrink behind the drapes.

                         GRACE
          Well, he offered, and I just couldn't
          refuse. His car overheated.

                         SHERIFF
          Oh?

                                                    (CONTINUED)

10   CONTINUED: (8)   10

Bobby turns to the Sheriff and forces a smile.

                        BOBBY
              Morning, officer.

                        SHERIFF
              Son.
                   (beat, to Grace)
              Little excitement out at the reservation
              this morning. Wayne and Dale Elkhart were
              up drinking all night and then Wayne starts
              chasing Dale around the desert with his
              shotgun. BIA handled it. I went by for
              backup.

                        GRACE
              Anybody hurt?

                        SHERIFF
              Hell, no. That Wayne can't shoot straight
              sober, much less drunk. He's lucky he
              didn't kill his own danged self.
                   (beat)
              Well, anyhow, you stay cool. Nice meeting
              you, son.

                        BOBBY
              Same here, officer.

The Sheriff drives on. Pause. They look at each other.

                        GRACE
              Well, I guess I could use some help
              carrying this box into the house. Not far.
              You could shower, get something cool to
              drink.

Bobby considers the offer, but there's not much considering to
do.

                        BOBBY
              Well, I could use something cool.

11   EXT. DESERT ROAD - DAY   11

BOBBY rides along with GRACE in her JEEP.

                        GRACE
              Where you coming from?

                        BOBBY
              All over. Chicago, Houston, Detroit. Just
              lately Dallas.

                                                    (CONTINUED)

                          GRACE
          You've been around.

                          BOBBY
          I guess I've got wander in my blood.

                          GRACE
          Where you headed?

                          BOBBY
          I don't know. I have to make a stop in
          Vegas. Business to finish. Then maybe
          I'll head to Santa Barbara. I might be
          able to pick up some action there.

                          GRACE
          So, what is it you do, Mister...?

                          BOBBY
          Cooper. Bobby Cooper. Oh you know, whatever
          pays best. Little bartending, used to teach
          tennis, played a little competition ...
          (drops it).

                          GRACE
          I never played tennis. You just travel
          around Bobby-- no direction, no steady
          work. You must like taking chances.

                          BOBBY
          If you're going to gamble, might as well
          play for high stakes.

                          GRACE
          What happens when you lose?

                          BOBBY
          I pack up and go somewhere else.

                          GRACE (wistfully)
          Somewhere else. I've never been anywhere
          else. Just once. Years ago. Went to the
          State Fair. It was nice, but it wasn't
          nothing.

                          BOBBY
          I couldn't stay in this place. I wouldn't.
          I'd just pick up, do whatever I had to do,
          and get out.

Grace looks to Bobby and smiles.

                                             (CONTINUED)

11   CONTINUED: (2)   11

                              GRACE
                    Sometimes I feel the exact same way.

12   INT. GRACE'S BEDROOM/BATHROOM - LATER - DAY   12

        BOBBY, naked, steps into the shower and turns on the water. It
        shoots from the shower head and cascades over his body. As the
        water falls over him we hear a Russian accented voice:

                              VOICE(V.O.)
                    I want my money.

        Bobby press his left hand against the white tile to steady
        himself. His hand is curled in such a way we cannot see his
        pinky or ring finger. Bobby leans back in the shower. Just as
        he does:

13   EXT. ALLEY - NIGHT   13

        It is raining hard. Matching the backwards motion of the last
        scene BOBBY is thrown violently against a brick wall, facing
        out.

                              VOICE(V.O.)
                    I want my money.

                              BOBBY
                    Look, I'll get the money! You don't want to
                    do this!

                              VOICE (V.O.)
                    Take two for now. One a week, punk...

        Bobby is being pressed against the wall by two muscular GOONS.
        Another MAN stands partially hidden behind the goon's frame.
        With one hand one goon flattens Bobby's hand against the brick,
        with his other he clips two fingers off with a GARDEN SHEAR. We
        see Bobby's face in agonizing pain, then he slides *screaming* to
        the ground until he is framed between the legs of the men.

        As Bobby clutches his left hand the rainwater runs in streaks
        down his ashen, blank face.

14   INT. GRACE'S BEDROOM/BATHROOM - MOMENTS LATER   14

        We see BOBBY's face reliving the experience as once again we
        hear the voice.

                              VOICE (V.O.)
                    Two weeks, asshole. Get the money or you
                    gonna lose your nose and ears.

                                                             (CONTINUED)

14   CONTINUED: 14

Bobby has slumped to the floor of the shower, looking to his
left hand, almost crying, unable to tolerate it. As a streak of
blood snakes down the white tile we see that the pinky and ring
FINGERS have been cut off at the joints.

15   INT. GRACE'S BEDROOM/BATHROOM - DAY   15

BOBBY, his hand rebandaged, is putting on his clothes.

                    BOBBY (to himself)
          You're still lucky.

As he does he looks at himself in the mirror. He bends to pick
up his shirt which is draped over the gym bag. As he lifts it we
can see, perhaps more closely than at the garage, that the bag is
3/4 filled with money. He closes the bag and stands. In the
MIRROR, hidden in the doorway, he sees GRACE watching him. Bobby
slows perceptibly, but does not try to hide himself. After a
moment Grace walks into the room carrying a glass of lemonade.

                    GRACE
          Thought you might like a refill on your lemonade.

Bobby takes the lemonade and drinks it down. He rubs the glass
against his forehead.

                    BOBBY
          That's good. Cools you right off.
          (tentatively) I saw you watching me.

                    GRACE
          I'm sorry. I didn't mean to.

                    BOBBY
          I didn't say it bothered me.

                    GRACE
          Did you like it; me watching you?

                    BOBBY
          I guess. I've got an ego same as any man.

                    GRACE
          Good, 'cause I liked what I saw.

Bobby gives a smile as devilish as it is pleasant. Grace slides
an ice cube from the glass between her lips. He notices a framed
picture of GRACE and an OLDER MAN.

                    BOBBY
          Nice place.

                                                    (CONTINUED)

                    GRACE
          Thank you.

Grace sits on the edge of the bed. Bobby indicates the picture,
ironic.

                    BOBBY
          Who's that, your father?

                    GRACE (without much thought)
          Stepfather...

                    BOBBY (coy)
          Got a boyfriend?

                    GRACE
          No. Not really.

Bobby senses she's lying but plays along.

                    BOBBY
          Must get kind of lonely for a woman living
          by herself in a big house.

                    GRACE
          I guess it must.

                    BOBBY
          What do you do anyway?

                    GRACE
          A little of this, a little of that. Mostly
          I tell fortunes.

                    BOBBY
          Where'd you learn to do that?

                    GRACE
          From my father. He was the tribe's shaman.

                    BOBBY
          A medicine man?

                    GRACE
          Those are white words, not ours.

                    BOBBY
          Nice house for a shaman's daughter. You
          must be good.

                    GRACE
          Come here.

(CONTINUED)

15   CONTINUED: (2)   15

Bobby goes to Grace and kneels before her. She takes his head
in her hands and looks deep into his eyes. Her voice goes
thick, but soft, like a morning fog.

                    GRACE
          There's something in your past; something
          you want to keep hidden. There's a pain.
          Something . . . someone you can't forget.
          And there is something you want very badly.
          It seems very far away to you, but you are
          determined, and you will do what you must
          to get it.

Bobby closes his hands on Grace's and takes them from his face.
He is more than slightly spooked by the accuracy of Grace's
reading.

                    BOBBY
          My face tell you all that?

                    GRACE
          It tells me what every face tells me.
          Everybody has a past, they have a pain, and
          they have something they want.
          (seductively) What is it you want?

                    BOBBY
          The same thing you do.

They silently stare into each other's eyes.

                    GRACE
          Really? I want to hang drapes.

Grace walks from the room. For a moment Bobby stares after her.
He takes an ice cube from his glass and crunches it in his
teeth.

16   INT. GRACE'S LIVING ROOM - DAY   16

GRACE is standing on a step ladder trying to hang the drapes.
BOBBY notices a photo of Grace with an older INDIAN WOMAN, her
mother?

                    GRACE
          Hold me.

Bobby stands behind her, gently places his hands on Grace's
waist.

                    GRACE
          Tighter. I won't break. You know girls are
          a lot tougher than men think.

                                              (CONTINUED)

16   CONTINUED: 16

Bobby holds her tighter as she finishes hanging the drapes. His
eyes are transfixed on her ass.

                    GRACE
          There. All done. Lift me down.

                    BOBBY
          What?

                    GRACE
          Lift me down.

Bobby lifts Grace down from the ladder. He holds her, his hands
around her waist.

                    GRACE
          You can let go of me now. I'm safe.(with
          a wicked smile) How do they look?

                    BOBBY
          Like you.

                    GRACE
          Beautiful?

                    BOBBY (kidding)
          Like they're made of polyester.

                    GRACE
          I like them. I was sick of looking at this
          room. I think they add a little life.

                    BOBBY
          Nothing like a little liveliness.

With a sexy pout Grace loads the next question.

                    GRACE
          No more drapes to hang. Now what should
          we do?

                    BOBBY
          I have an idea.

                    GRACE
          And what would that be?

Bobby steps close to Grace and takes her by the shoulders. He
pulls her to him and presses his lips hard to hers. Grace
doesn't respond.

                    BOBBY
          All right, Grace. No more games.

                                              (CONTINUED)

                    GRACE (innocently)
          Games?

                    BOBBY
          You flirt with me, then you run cold. You
          lead me on, then slap me down. I don't go
          for being jerked around.

                    GRACE
          Really? And what game did you want to
          play? You carry my box for me, and I fall
          into bed with you?

Bobby grabs up his pack.

                    BOBBY
          I think I can find my own way back to
          into town.

                    GRACE
          Maybe I like to find out about a man first.
          Maybe I like to know what he's made of.

                    BOBBY
          I'm just flesh and blood, baby. That and a
          few memories of bad women; just like most
          guys. But you already know that. You read
          my mind, remember? Thanks for the lemonade.

Bobby turns to leave.

                    GRACE
          You never did answer my question.

                    BOBBY
          Still playing?

                    GRACE
          That's not an answer. What is it you want?

                    BOBBY
          You know what I want.

                    GRACE
          Maybe I just want to hear you say it.

For a beat Bobby stands and stares hard at Grace. His pack
slides from his shoulder and thuds on the floor. With great
determination, like a beast closing for the kill, Bobby moves
for her. Grace stands firm, ready for him; her head tilts back.
Her breath comes deep and hard.

Just as Bobby is about to reach her, just as he is about to take her, he is stopped dead by the booming voice of JAKE McKENNA.

                    JAKE (O.S.)
          Grace!

Bobby turns to face Jake: An older man, still large and formidable for his age.

                    GRACE (nonplussed)
          Jake. I thought you...

                    JAKE
          Who the hell is this!?

                    BOBBY
          Who the hell are you?

                    JAKE
          I'm her husband.

                    BOBBY (shocked whisper)
          Husband . . .?

                    JAKE
          Now who the hell are you, and it better be
          good, or God help me I'll break you in
          half.

                    BOBBY
          Easy, chief. I... I was helping your wife.
          I met her in town. She needed a hand with
          her drapes. That's all.

                    JAKE
          Didn't much look like you were hanging
          drapes.

                    BOBBY
          I swear to you that's all that happened. I
          haven't so much as set foot in your
          bedroom.

                    JAKE
          A lot that means.

                    BOBBY
          Grace, tell him.

Grace says nothing. She picks up a glass of lemonade and sips at it coolly.

                                                      (CONTINUED)

                              BOBBY
                    Damn it, Grace! Tell him.

                              GRACE (coyly)
                    If he says that's what happened, Jake, it
                    must be true.

                              JAKE
                    Oh yeah, and I suppose you didn't have
                    anything to do with it Grace, he just
                    wandered up here by hisself. I got a mind
                    to put you over my knee and paddle your
                    ass *raw*!

                              BOBBY (to Grace)
                    You bitch! Is this what it's all about? You
                    sucker me up here so you can watch the two
                    of us beat the shit out of each other over
                    you? You both... Forget it! (heads for the
                    door)

                              JAKE
                    Where you going!

                              BOBBY (exiting)
                    'Scuse me, you want to take my head off,
                    mister. I won't even try to stop you. I
                    deserve it for being an idiot. But if
                    you're not, I think I'll be on my way...
                    Ow!

Jake punches him in the nose.

                              JAKE
                    You can't just walk in here and walk out,
                    you sonufabitch! I'm gonna tear you a new
                    asshole!

                              BOBBY
                    You broke my nose!

                              JAKE
                    It ain't broke.

It probably isn't, but it bleeds. Bobby feels the blood and then
sees it on his shirt.

                              BOBBY
                    Goddamn it! I'm... you're lucky I don't sue
                    you.

                              JAKE (opens the door)
                    Get goin' Junior.

16   CONTINUED: (5)   16

Bobby glares back at Grace who gives him a maddening little smile.

> BOBBY
> You people are crazy!

He storms out holding his nose.

17   EXT. DESERT ROAD - LATER - DAY   17

BOBBY, holding a handkerchief to his nose which has stopped bleeding, hauling his bag on his shoulder, walks back to town along the side of the road. Already he is caked with a mixture of sweat and dust, looking up at the relentless sun that beats down on him.

> BOBBY
> Fuckin' shithole!

A CADILLAC slows beside him, JAKE driving.

> BOBBY
> What the fuck do you want?

> JAKE
> I'll give you a lift, son. Too hot to be walking... People die out here, y'know.

Bobby continues walking.

> JAKE
> Aw, you're not still upset about that love tap, are you? If I meant you real trouble, I'd have given it to you by now. Get in, lad. Come on. Get in.

Bobby gets in.

> JAKE
> After you huffed off, Grace lied so bad, I got so pissed off, I pulled down her pants to paddle her ass raw and finger-fucked it instead. Sorry I lost my cool like that. It's a funny thing, women.

> BOBBY
> Yeah...

> JAKE
> Say, what happened to your hand?

                    BOBBY
Accident.

                    JAKE
You've got to be--

                    BOBBY
Yeah, I know. More careful.

                    JAKE
I guess we've never been introduced proper.
Jake McKenna.

                    BOBBY
That's a solid name.

                    JAKE
I'm a solid man.

                    BOBBY
Bobby Cooper.

                    JAKE
"Bobby Cooper." What brings you to
Superior, Coop?

                    BOBBY
An overheated car.

                    JAKE
Oh? Darrell taking good care of you?

                    BOBBY
Darrell's a moron.

                    JAKE (laughs)
Yeah, he sure is a character. You need any
help with that car now?... Where you
headed?

                    BOBBY
California...

                    JAKE
Live there?

                    BOBBY
Got work. I know a man who's got a boat.
Wants me to sail it for him.

                    JAKE
You a sailor man? That'd be the life.
Drive across the country, step on a boat
                    (MORE)

(CONTINUED)

17   CONTINUED: (2)   17

> JAKE (cont'd)
> and just sail away. A man could pretty
> well disappear like that. Just sail away
> until all he was was a memory. I guess a
> little place like this would just be a dot
> on a map to you after awhile.

> BOBBY
> I hope so. (beat) Listen, McKenna about
> your wife: If I had known she was
> married--

> JAKE
> It wouldn't have made a difference to you,
> now would it? Not a wit. Do you know why?
> Because you're a man without scruples.

> BOBBY
> Wait a second--

> JAKE
> Ah, I can smell it on you.

Jake wipes his hand across the back of Bobby's neck and holds it
to his nose.

> BOBBY
> Hey!

> JAKE
> That's the sweat of a man who hasn't an
> honest bone in his body. Don't be
> offended, lad. A man who's got no ethics
> is a free man. I envy that. Beside, how
> can I blame you? That Grace sure has a
> mind of her own, and a body to match, don't
> she? Eh?

Jake nudges Bobby who smiles a nervous smile.

> JAKE
> She does at that. I knew when I married
> her she was a free spirit. A woman with
> her looks and a man my age; what was I to
> expect? But you see a woman like that in a
> town like this and you don't think, you do.
> So, I married her. What are you to do, eh?
> Women.

> BOBBY
> Can't live with them, and you can't shoot
> 'em.

Jake looks at Bobby, his lips curled into a sly smile.

(CONTINUED)

                    JAKE
          "You can't shoot 'em!" I like that.
          (laughs) I bet she led you on good, didn't
          she? Taking you up to the house to hang
          drapes. Oh that's a good one. Bet she had
          you hard as a rock wiggling her ass in your
          face. I bet you just wanted to pull down
          her pants and hog her out. Then me busting
          in like some wild bear. Ha! Bet you had a
          fire going under you.

                    BOBBY
          Like you don't know.

                    JAKE
          Mad like a dog in heat, I bet you were. I
          can tell you got a temper on you.

Bobby gives a little laugh.

                    JAKE
          Bet you just wanted to snap her neck right
          then, didn't you? Bet you just wanted to
          kill her.

Bobby starts to laugh heartily. Jake joins in, then stops
abruptly.

                    JAKE
          Would you?

                    BOBBY
          Would I what?

                    JAKE
          Would you kill her?

Bobby starts to laugh. Bobby stops laughing.

                    BOBBY
          Why would I kill her?

                    JAKE
          Because I'm sick and tired of her little
          games. Because you could do it and drift
          away on your boat and no one would ever see
          you again. Because I've got a
          fifty-thousand dollar life insurance policy
          on her, and I would be more than happy to
          give the man who does her in a good chunk
          of it.

                                            (CONTINUED)

For a moment Bobby sits in silence not sure of what to make of the offer.

                    BOBBY
          I've done a few things but I'm not a
          murderer, Mr. McKenna.

                    JAKE
          How do you know if you've never tried?

                    BOBBY
          This is a joke, right? You just want to
          rattle me. Right?

They reach town and Jake stops the car near a small GROCERY STORE.

                    JAKE
          That's right. Nothing but a joke. That's
          all.

Bobby gets out of the car. With a big smile Jake says:

                    JAKE
          Enjoy your stay, lad.

Jake speeds away. Bobby looks after him.

                    BOBBY
          Who *are* these people.

18   INT. SMALL GROCERY STORE - LATER   18

The store is small and dark and empty save for a tiny, older Mexican WOMAN who is behind the counter. BOBBY enters.

                    BOBBY
          Got any cold soda?

                    WOMAN
          Eh?

                    BOBBY
          Soda. You got any soda?

                    WOMAN
          Hablar slowly, por favor. My ingles no es
          bien.

                    BOBBY
          Soda. You know.

Bobby cups his hand and brings it to his mouth pantomiming.

                                              (CONTINUED)

                              WOMAN
                    Oh.   Something to eat.   Si.

She holds up a pack of Twinkies.

                              BOBBY
                    Not eat.   Drink.   What the fuck is drink in
                    Spanish . . . uh, agua?

The old woman's eyes widen.   She starts to scream, but quickly
clamps her hands over her mouth.   For a moment Bobby thinks the
woman is screaming at what he has said.   Then, as if he feels a
presence behind him, Bobby turns slowly to face the TWO
tough-looking, unshaven, tattoo-covered BIKERS.   One holds a
gun.

                              BIKER
                    That's right, lady.   Keep it in you and
                    nobody gets hurt.   That goes for you too,
                    stud.   Gimmie the money.   Now!

                              WOMAN
                    Eh?

                         SECOND BIKER
                    The dinero, Senora.   Hand it over.

Bobby shifts his weight trying to hide his pack behind his back.

The woman goes to an old-fashioned cash register and rings it
open.   She hands the money to the biker.

                              BIKER
                    That's it?   Lady, I got kids to put through
                    school.

                              WOMAN
                    Es all I have.

The biker turns to Bobby.

                              BIKER
                    Okay, pal.   Whatcha got? Give it, now.

Bobby pulls a thick wad in cash ($1,000 plus) from his pant
pocket, tosses it on the counter.

                         BIKER (thumbing through it, impressed)
                    Nice...Just who *are* *you* beautiful? What
                    else you got for papa?

Bobby makes a show of pulling out his wallet, flings it to him.

                                                      (CONTINUED)

> BIKER
> Better...you're getting tasty. Now toss the
> bag, sweetie.

> BOBBY
> It's just books.

> BIKER
> I'm a reader. Toss it.

> BOBBY (an entreaty)
> It's personal things...family things.

> BIKER
> How touching...I like family values. Give
> it to me.

Bobby takes an unsteady breath.

> BOBBY
> No.

> BIKER
> No?

> SECOND BIKER
> Hey man, forget it. Come on.

> BIKER
> No?

> WOMAN
> Senor, give him the bag.

> BIKER
> That's all right. He doesn't want to give
> me the bag...

> SECOND BIKER
> He's fucking with you man. Shoot him.

> BIKER (cont'd)
> ...he doesn't have to give me the bag.

The biker grabs Bobby's bag. Bobby flinches in anticipation of a
shot but refuses to let go of the bag. The biker swings the gun
hard, clipping Bobby across the forehead. Bobby falls against
the counter and to the floor. The woman starts to scream. The
biker grabs up the pack, then, looking back at the woman, sees a
ring on her finger. He grabs her hand and pulls at the ring.
The woman screams wildly.

                         SECOND BIKER
               Let's go, man.

                         BIKER
               A little extra never hurt, Benji, would you
               just relax.

                         WOMAN
               No! No! My wedding ring.

He pulls the ring from the woman's finger and pushes her back.
With Bobby's bag slung over his shoulder he turns to leave.

                         BIKER
               Now we go.

                         WOMAN
               You go to El Diablo!

From beneath the counter the woman pulls a shotgun. The woman
fires A SHOT that rips through the bag and into the back of the
biker. He falls to the ground, very dead, amid a shower of
blood and shredded money.

                         SECOND BIKER
               Bugger! You bitch!

The Second Biker now sees the money floating all over the place
out of the torn bag. His eyes go big with greed as he FIRES at
the old woman, who ducks behind the counter.

The Biker grabs for the bag and what's left of the money, not
expecting the feisty old lady to pop up and unload her SECOND
BLAST into him and the bag.

Whatever was left of the money on the first round is now gone to
shreds along with the bag and the Biker who is very dead.

Bobby is staggered, crawls towards the shreds.

                         WOMAN (cursing in Spanish)
               Hijos de puta. Bayan a comer su propia
               mierda en el infierno. (TRANSLATION: Sons
               of bitches. Go eat your own shit in hell).

She comes around the counter to his side as he grabs his wallet
and the $1000 cash roll from the dead biker's pants.

                         WOMAN
               I call the sheriff.

                         BOBBY
               No! No police.

                                              (CONTINUED)

18   CONTINUED: (4)   18

Bobby gives her a hundred dollars.

                         WOMAN
               A hundred dollars? No police?

Bobby gives her some more cash. She looks at him. Finally he
gives her the entire wad.

                         BOBBY
               No police until I leave.

Bobby stumbles from the store as the screen burns a bright white.

                                             FADE TO:

19   EXT. STREET - LATER   19

     BOBBY, dazed and holding his head, sits on the ground next to a
     SPIGOT that is dripping water. He cups his hands under the
     water and splashes it against his face, lightly wiping the cut
     above his eye. The SHERIFF'S CAR goes wailing by on the main
     drag. Recoiling from being spotted, Bobby tries to take another
     drink. A SCORPION crawls out of the faucet. He jumps back.

20   EXT. HARLIN'S GARAGE - LATER   20

     DARRELL is leaning under the hood of a car working on its engine
     as BOBBY walks up.

                         BOBBY
               Hey.

                         DARRELL
               Hey, your . . . what the hell happened to
               you?

                         BOBBY
               Nothing.

                         DARRELL
               Don't look like nothing.

                         BOBBY
               Just banged my head. It was an accident.

                         DARRELL
               Another accident? You got to be more
               careful.

Bobby rolls his eyes. Then notices the front fenders have been
removed.

                                             (CONTINUED)

                              BOBBY
          What the hell happened to my car?

                              DARRELL
          Bottom hose was shot too. Rotted clear
          through. Had to put a new one in. Runs like
          a dream now.

                              BOBBY (suspicious)
          How much?

                              DARRELL
          Well . . . you got your parts, you got your
          labor . . . let's call it a hundred-fifty
          bucks.

                              BOBBY
          How much!?

                              DARRELL
          Hundred-fifty.

                              BOBBY
          To replace a goddamn radiator hose!?

                              DARRELL
          A goddamn radiator hose in a
          sixty-four-and-a-half Mustang. You know
          how long it took me to find that hose?

                              BOBBY
          About an hour and a half, because that's
          all the longer I've been gone.

                              DARRELL
          Actually, it's been about three hours.
          You're the one thinks that car's so damn
          fancy. What you expect but fancy damn
          prices?

                              BOBBY
          That's a Ford, not a Ferrari. You going to
          tell me no one else in this shit hole
          drives a Ford?

                              DARRELL
          "That's not just a Ford, that's a
          sixty-four-and-a-half Mustang."

                              BOBBY
          What's that got to do with the radiator hose?

                                              (CONTINUED)

>   DARRELL
> I don't know, but "it's the reason I'm living
> here and you're just passing through." Now you
> owe me a hundred-fifty dollars.

>   BOBBY
> It might as well be fifteen-hundred
> dollars, because I don't have the money.

>   DARRELL
> Then you ain't gonna have the car.

>   BOBBY
> Listen, man. I got rolled half an hour ago
> for everything I had.

Bobby digs through his bloodied wallet, trying to hide it from
Darrell. He fishes out a five dollar bill. Then digs out a
bloody one dollar bill from his pocket.

>   BOBBY
> I've got five...six dollars.

Darrell snatches the five from him and adds it to a thick wad of
greasy bills he carries in his overalls.

>   DARRELL
> Then you're only a hundred-forty-five in
> the hole. You can keep that dollar. Now
> why don't you just take your American
> Express Gold Card, and call that guy with
> the big schnooz on TV and have him send you
> the money lickity split.

>   BOBBY
> I don't have a goddamn credit card.

>   DARRELL
> Now that's too bad. I sure hope you know
> how to wash dishes or shovel shit 'cause
> you're gonna have to work this one off.

Bobby proffers his Movado watch.

>   BOBBY
> Look, I got a Movado. It's worth at least
> seven, eight hundred. You could sell it for
> that.

>   DARRELL (studying it)
> Who the hell to? Shit, can't see no
> numbers.

                                                    (CONTINUED)

20   CONTINUED: (3)   20

                    BOBBY
          You don't need numbers. That's why it's
          expensive. Look at the gold.

Darrell doubts that, shakes his head.

                    DARRELL
          ...got no day, got no date. Probably ain't
          worth a duck's fart (proffers his own
          watch). This one here cost me $3.75 and
          it's got every doodad you can imagine. No
          sir I'll stick with this (walks away).

                    BOBBY
          You son of a bitch! I'll have my lawyers
          shut you down.

                    DARRELL
          You ain't got no credit card but you got a
          lawyer. Sweet talk me all you want. Didn't
          you read the sign? It says...

                    BOBBY
          What sign? Fuck the sign. I want my car.

                    DARRELL
          I want my hundred and forty-five dollars.

Bobby stands his ground for a moment as if deciding whether or
not to fight for the car, then wheels and walks away.

Darrell looks at him, smirks

21   INT. TRUCK STOP/DINER - LATER   21

It is a little worn diner-type stop one would find on most any
open road: Counter with stools, laminated menus, a Wurlitzer in
the corner belching out country TUNES. Business is slow but
it's the only restaurant in town. There is a SHORT ORDER COOK in
the kitchen, and FLO, a hard-looking waitress is behind the
counter. A couple of regular drivers, ED and BOYD, are seated
on the stools, Boyd is flipping a coin.

                    ED
          One-hundred-thirteen degrees. That was
          back in July of forty-seven. That afternoon
          it dropped down to forty three! True story.

                    BOYD
          One time last year I remember it went from
          98 to 23 same day. Wind, black clouds come
          out like...

                                              (CONTINUED)

21   CONTINUED: 21

BOBBY comes out of the men's room and sits at the end of the
counter. He has cleaned himself up a bit but still looks like a
mess. He buries his face in the menu.

                    BOBBY
          You got a beer?

                    FLO
          What kind?

                    BOBBY
          Beck's.

                    FLO
          No Beck's. A-1, Coors...

                    BOBBY
          Heineken?

                    FLO
          No, we ain't got no Heineken. We got
          Miller.

                    BOBBY
          Genuine Draft?

                    FLO
          No. Just plain ol' Miller. Now you can
          fuckin' take it or your can fuckin' leave
          it.

                    BOBBY
          I'll fuckin' take it. To go.

                    SHORT ORDER COOK
          Flo, cheeseburger bleedin'.

                    FLO
          I'll be right back with that beer.

Flo moves off.

                    BOBBY
          ...and a waitress named Flo. Christ.

As Bobby stares at the money on the counter in front of him, he
hears, from somewhere outside the diner, the sound of a POLICE
RADIO crackling. He now feels something against his foot. He
looks down and sees a CAT rubbing against his leg. He gives it
a good kick sending it sliding across the floor with a screech.

                    BOBBY
          Fucking cat.

                                                    (CONTINUED)

In the background, two teenagers sit a booth. TOBY looks the
part of a local, wearing jeans and a white T-shirt. His hair is
cropped close and he looks to be a senior in high school. His
girl, JENNY, is nondescript, neither ugly not beautiful. She is
the kind of girl most guys would pass without a second look.
Toby gets up from his booth and goes to the bathroom. After he
is gone Jenny walks to Bobby.

                    JENNY
          Hey, Mister. You gotta quarter for the
          juke?

                    BOBBY
          What?

                    JENNY
          I wanna play a song on the juke. You got a
          quarter?

Bobby looks at Jenny, then picks a quarter from his winnings and
flips it to her. He can't resist putting a little charm into it.

                    JENNY
          What happened to your hand?

                    BOBBY
          I cut it shaving; I know, I gotta be more
          careful.

                    JENNY
          Got any requests?

                    BOBBY
          That country shit all sounds the same to
          me.

                    JENNY
          How about I pick one out for you?

Bobby half smiles. Jenny plays a song. Patsy Cline's "Your
Cheatin' Heart." Jenny takes up a stool next to Bobby's.

                    JENNY
          You like Patsy Cline? I just love her.
          How come, I wonder, she don't put out no
          more new records.

                    BOBBY
          Cause she's dead.

                    JENNY
          Gee, that's sad. Don't that make you sad?

                                            (CONTINUED)

                    BOBBY
          I've had time to get over it.

                    JENNY
          You're not from around here, are you?
          Where you from?

                    BOBBY
          Oz.

                    JENNY
          You ain't from Oz. Oz is in that movie.

                    BOBBY
          You're too quick for me.

Toby walks back into the room. He looks at Jenny. He looks at
Bobby. He looks at Jenny talking to Bobby. He loses it.

                    TOBY
          No....No....No I'm seeing but I'm not
          believin'...Stop the wedding. This can't
          be. Hey! What are you doing with my girl?

Bobby says nothing, ignoring Toby.

                    TOBY
          I axed you a question.

                    JENNY
          Aw, Toby, we weren't doing nothing. We was
          just talking.

                    TOBY
          You shut your mouth, girl, and get back
          over to our table. (to Bobby) Now, I'm not
          going to axe you again, Mister. What were
          you doing with my girl?

                    BOBBY
          I wasn't doing anything.

                    TOBY
          That's not the way it looked to me. Looked
          to me like you was trying to make time with
          her.

                    BOBBY
          Make time? Is everybody in this town on
          drugs?

        JENNY
Honest, Toby. I just axed him for a
quarter for the jukebox.

        TOBY
Stay out of this, Jenny. We got man's
business to take care of. I ain't never
taken no drugs, mister, and ...

        BOBBY
Then maybe you should've. Look, pal, I
wasn't making a play for your girl.

        TOBY
You expect me to believe that?

        BOBBY
I don't care what you believe as long as
you leave me alone.

        TOBY
Mister, I'm calling you out.

        BOBBY
What? You want to fight? Over her?

Bobby looks Jenny over.

        FLO
Toby, you go finish your soda and leave the
man alone.

        TOBY (to Bobby)
You know who I am? Toby N. Tucker.
Everyone round here call me TNT. You know
why?

        BOBBY
Let's see...they're not very imaginative?

        TOBY
'Cause I'm just like dynamite. And when I
go off, somebody gets hurt.

        BOBBY
Fine. I was making time with your girl.
Now I'm scared to death and I learned my
lesson. Now can you go away?

        TOBY
Not before I settle with you, chickenshit!

(CONTINUED)

                  BOBBY
Christ, I don't believe this!

                  TOBY
Stand up.

                  BOBBY
I wasn't hitting on your girl!

                  TOBY
Stand up, Mister, or I'll beat you where
you sit.

Bobby sits for a beat. He doesn't need a fight with Toby now
with his damaged hand nor does he need to be noticed either. He
sits there.

                  FLO
Toby, you stop it now! Can't you see he's
got a hurt hand?

                  TOBY
Don't you never mind, Flo. This is gonna
be over real quick.

Reluctantly Bobby rises, facing off against Toby, each clenching
their fist and waiting for the other to make the first move.
The tension builds. We see it on the faces of Jenny, Flo and
the regulars. Just then the record on the juke ends and the
needle scratches off. There is the crackle of a police radio as
the door to the diner opens and SHERIFF VIRGIL POTTER walks in.
The tension eases. Toby, mindful of the sheriff, steps close to
Bobby and whispers menacingly into his ear.

                  TOBY
You're lucky, Mister. Don't think it's
over. I called you out and I'm gonna see
this through. You hear me? (to Jenny)
Come on, girl. I got half a mind to make
you walk home.

Toby takes Jenny by the arm and pulls her out of the diner.

                  FLO
My lord, that little baby of yours Virgil,
has gotten cuter'n a bunny's nose.

                  SHERIFF
What was that all about?

                  FLO
You know how that Toby is. Thinks every
man he sees is after his Jenny.

                              SHERIFF
          More like Jenny is after every man she
          sees.

                              FLO (to Bobby)
          You pay Toby no mind. He just likes to
          show off for his girl. Give him a couple
          of hours, he'll cool off. Still want that
          beer?

                              BOBBY (tense, seeing the Sheriff)
          I'll take it to go.

Bobby holds his hand to his face to cover the cut on his
forehead.

                              ED
          How's it with you, Sheriff?

                              SHERIFF
          Already started out bad. Couple of bikers
          from out of town tried to knock over
          Jamilla's grocery store this morning. It
          was a real shootout.

                              BOYD
          What happened?

                              SHERIFF
          The old witch killed 'em both.

                              ED
          Holy shit!

                              FLO
          Poor thing. Is she all right?

                              SHERIFF
          Sure, when the sons of bitches tried to
          steal her wedding ring. That's when she
          started shooting. Can't blame her. The
          ring was all Carlos left her when he died.
          Store's a mess.

                              BOYD
          It's the desert. That's what it is. The
          desert makes everybody crazy. Ain't that
          right, Sheriff? People go crazy out here.

(CONTINUED)

                              ED
               Come on, Boyd. I've got to make tracks.
               That yogurt's got to make Santa Fe before
               it spoils.

                              BOYD
               Dr. Pepper don't have that problem.

Ed and Boyd toss a few bills on the counter and exit. Flo
stands near the cash register with Bobby's beer.

                              FLO
               I can't open off-sale for you, sugar.

Bobby pays for the beer ($1.75). Flo opens the register.

                              FLO
               Let me get your change.

                              SHERIFF
               Flo, I'm just gonna help myself to a refill
               on the coffee.

The Sheriff reaches across the counter for the pot.

                              FLO
               You be careful now, Virgil.

Just as the words leave Flo's mouth the Sheriff spills the pot.
It shatters against the floor spilling hot coffee everywhere.
Flo runs over to him.

                              SHERIFF
               Son of a bitch!

                              FLO
               Virgil! Now look at what you done! Are
               you all right?

                              SHERIFF
               I think I burned my gun hand!

As Flo bends to wipe the counter, Virgil touches her intimately.

                              SHERIFF (Cont'd)
               How 'bout we put something soft on it
               later? (a look)

                              FLO
               (quietly) I could put some butter on it,
               hon'. (Her normal abrasive voice) It'd
               serve you right, you asshole. Put it under
                              (MORE)

21 CONTINUED: (8)   21

                              FLO (cont'd)
                    some cold water. Joe, run get a mop and
                    clean this fuckin' mess up.

While everyone is distracted Bobby notices that the register
drawer has been left open. He looks around to make sure he is
not being watched. Slowly he eases his hand towards the drawer.
It gets closer and closer. As he is about to grab the money
there, the cat - the same one he kicked away earlier - hisses
and claws at his hand. Bobby jumps back startled.

                              FLO
                    Shasta! Now why'd you go and scare the
                    nice man like that? Sorry about that,
                    mister. Let's see, you want $3.25. (gives
                    it to him) You try to have a nice day now,
                    would you?

                              BOBBY
                    Sure, I'll try.

With the Sheriff occupied, and the Mexican Jose mopping the
floor, Bobby exits.

22 EXT. PHONE BOOTH - STREET - DAY   22

BOBBY begs on the phone.

                              BOBBY
                    Cici? Cici, it's Bobby...Bobby
                    Cooper...Yeah, look, I know it's been a
                    while, but I'm kind of in a
                    jam...yeah...One-hundred-fifty
                    dollars...That's a lie. I called you on
                    your birthday..Two years ago...I can't help
                    it if you didn't get the message. Cici,
                    honey, I don't want to argue. I need you to
                    wire me the money...Because they're fucking
                    going to *KILL ME*! I didn't steal your
                    CD's...Yeah, well where's my Mr. Coffee.
                    Cici...Cici...

Bobby slams the phone.

                              BOBBY
                    Bitch. Cunt.

                                                       JUMP CUT TO:

23 EXT. SAME PHONE BOOTH -STREET- DAY   23

BOBBY is on another call, circling a local sports page betting
line.

                                                       (CONTINUED)

CONTINUED:

                    BOBBY
         73-11, this is Pluto. What's the line on
         Dallas?

                  GAMBLER'S VOICE
         Pluto. Fucking deadbeat. We heard about
         you. You owe "the commie" 13 dimes, why you
         tryin' to get in my office? Lose this
         fuckin' number.

                    BOBBY
         Mike...Mike...you asshole.

                  GAMBLER'S VOICE
         Mike who?
              (hangs up)

Bobby, frustrated, clicks off.

                           JUMP CUT TO:

24   INT. MR. ARKADY'S OFFICE - DAY   24

It is the kind of cheesy, temporary office one would expect to find in a Las Vegas apartment building overlooking the DOWNTOWN STRIP. MR. ARKADY, dressed in a silk suit with conspicuous jewelry, sits behind his desk eating lunch and cleaning his nails. SERGEI, his goon in a shiny polyester shirt, hovers over his boss helping feed and manicure him. These are the TWO MEN from Bobby's earlier FLASHBACK. They are dangerous in an endearing way. Sergei answers the phone. In the background is a very voluptuous female, obviously from the Middle East. SOFIA.

                  SERGEI
         Da?

                  MR. ARKADY
         Sergei, what are you, a Neanderthal? How
         many times do I have to tell you? You
         answer a phone "hello," not "da."

                  SERGEI (nods yes)
         Sorry, Mr.Arkady.(into phone)"Hello?"

                  OPERATOR(V.O.)
         I have a collect call from Bobby Cooper.
         Will you accept the charges?

                  SERGEI
         Mr. Arkady, deadbeat Cooper's calling.

Mr. Arkady doesn't acknowledge him.

                           (CONTINUED)

24   CONTINUED: 24

                              SERGEI
                    He's calling collect.

At this Mr. Arkady's head springs up. He snatches the phone
from Sergei.

                    MR. ARKADY (overly sweet)
                    Bobby, what a surprise. I expected to be
                    seeing you, not talking to you over the
                    phone.

                                              INTERCUTS TO:

25   EXT. PHONE BOOTH - STREET   25

        BOBBY on the phone.

                              BOBBY
                    I know, Mr. Arkadin. I know. I was on my
                    way to you, it's just . . . what a day I've
                    had. I know I'm coming up with a highly
                    improbable story, and I know you're not
                    going to believe this, but this ...is...
                    what happened. I had the money, I swear I
                    had it. I was on my way to Vegas when my
                    car breaks down in the middle of nowhere.

Mr. Arkady cleans his nails completely disinterested in what
Bobby is saying.

                              MR. ARKADY
                    That's a shame, Bobby. A real shame.

                              BOBBY
                    And that's not the half of it, Mr.
                    Arkadin...

                              MR. ARKADY
                    "Arkady"

                              BOBBY
                    Right, Mr. Arkady. And that's not the half
                    of it. I got your money, and I go into this
                    little grocery store in this hicktown to
                    get something to eat and then... well, it
                    gets *robbed*!

                              MR. ARKADY
                    ...And let me guess. This robber -- he
                    gets your money.

                                              (CONTINUED)

                    BOBBY
No. Two of them. Two robbers. And they *both*
get nailed... get shot by the old lady.

                    MR. ARKADY
The old lady?

                    BOBBY
With a *shotgun*! She kills *both* of 'em,
and... and the money in my bag gets all
shredded to bloody pieces. Not one bill is
left alive. I mean, what are the odds?

                    MR. ARKADY (beat, dry)
Pretty long, Bobby.

                    BOBBY
Mr. Arkady, honest, I had to beat it outta
there before the cops showed. So now I
don't have a cent to my name. I can't even
get my car out of the garage. I tell you,
Mister... (pause) if it weren't for bad
luck I wouldn't have any fuckin' luck at
all, you know? (beat, waits) So, I was
wondering if you could wire me a hundred
fifty-dollars so I could get my car out of
this garage, see? The bus depot here has a
Western Union thing. And of course I'll
pay it back with the rest of the money.

                    MR. ARKADY (V.O.)
Which you don't have.

                    BOBBY
But which I can get. No problem. Look, I
can sell my car in Vegas. Blue book it's
worth 16 at least. I just need the 150,
uh...

Sergei looks like he's ready to pound heads.

                    MR. ARKADY (pause)
Where are you?

                    BOBBY (hopeful)
Uh...a little shithole in Arizona called
Superior. About 200 miles east of Phoenix.

                    MR. ARKADY (pausing, V.O.)
Superior, hunh?

Bobby suddenly feeling suspicious.

                                      (CONTINUED)

CONTINUED: (2)

                         BOBBY (V.O.)
              Yeah, if you could send it care of...

                         MR. ARKADY
              ...Now, let me get this straight. Two years
              you give me problems with your fuckin'
              payoffs. Now you owe me thirteen-thousand
              dollars, you call me - collect - then ask
              me to wire you one-hundred-fifty dollars
              just so you can get your car fixed.

                         BOBBY(V.O.)
              A hundred-forty-five would probably cover it.

                         MR. ARKADY
              A hundred and . . . Now you listen to me
              you deadbeat little punk: I don't care if
              you got hit by a truck and run over by a
              steamroller. You owe me thirteen-thousand
              dollars and I want it. I don't care how
              you get it, or where from, but I want it on
              my desk tomorrow, or I'll show you what
              real bad luck is.

              Sergei snaps a pencil he's holding in his hand, which goes
              flying by Arkady's head, forcing him to duck.

                         MR. ARKADY
              Do you understand me you little fuck?

                         BOBBY (snaps)
              Oh, fuck you too!

                         MR. ARKADY
              What'd you say to me!

                         BOBBY
              Shit I'm sorry!...you can't believe the
              strain I'm under. I'm just under a lot of
              strain here.

              There is a sharp silence at the other end. Bobby waits.

                         MR. ARKADY
              Bobby, you owed me that 'bread' 4 weeks
              ago. Now you tell me you want another week.
              That's 5 weeks, Bobby. That's also 5
              fingers, cause you and I know it's a finger
              a week Bobby. So you got balls. Good--now
              you come here tomorrow and you talk to me
              real nice and maybe I don't take the other
              3 fingers you owe me, you see? Tomorrow --
                              (MORE)

25   CONTINUED: (3)   25

                        MR. ARKADY (cont'd)
          and Bobby, don't make me come look for you,
          okay...have nice day.

He hands the phone back to Sergei.

                        SERGEI (into phone)
          You got that? -- have nice day (hangs up).

                        MR. ARKADY
          The nerva that piece of shit! And look at
          you, you Neanderthal -- don't you fuckin'
          break pencils, you goombah!

                        SOFIA
          Finger? What are you, a faggot? In my
          country a man don't pay we cut off his
          head.

Arkady motions Sergei to come close.

                        MR. ARKADY
          Get your ass down to this Superior,
          Arizona. Bring me this Bobby Cooper. I
          don't think he got the lesson. This is your
          last chance, Sergei.

                        SERGEI
          Da.

26   EXT. STREET - DAY   26

BOBBY, desperate, stares at the bandage of his wounded hand. It
throbs, holding the phone to his ear.

We hear an OPERATOR'S VOICE:

                        OPERATOR(V.O.)
          Hello?

                        BOBBY
          Hello?

                        OPERATOR(V.O.)
          Are you finished with your call?

                        BOBBY
          Yeah.

                        OPERATOR(V.O.)
          Please deposit an additional seventy-five
          cents.

Bobby slams the phone against the hook.

                                                      (CONTINUED)

26   CONTINUED: 26

                              BOBBY
              Goddamn rat's ass fuck! Shit! Damn! Damn!
              Damn!

He marches from the phone booth, past an old HARDWARE STORE. The
phone falls from the hook and we hear a recorded voice:

                              VOICE(V.O.)
              Thank you for using AT&T.

In the store window, Bobby notices a set of garden shears for
sale.

27   EXT. EMPTY STREET - LATER DAY   27

BOBBY walks a bit going nowhere in particular. Looking at his
watch thinking of Mr. Arkady, he shields himself with one hand
from the sun. At the side of an old building, in the bit of
shade it throws, he twists at the beer cap which sticks and
won't turn. Bobby tries again twisting harder -- too hard -- as
the cap jerkily twists off, cutting into his hand as it rotates.
Bobby yells in pain. At the same time the beer comes foaming
from the bottle and spills onto his sleeve. The bottle slips
from his wet fingers and crashes on the ground, emptying. He
clutches his bleeding hand, pissed.

                              BOBBY
              Fuck! Fuck! Fuck! I hate this fuckin' town!
              I hate it! Do you hear me?
                    (no answer)
              Get me outta here, please. I gotta get out
              of this place.

As if in answer, a JEEP drives by on the main street. GRACE
looks pretty hot up there in the driver's seat, her eyes, behind
sunglasses, flicking over him but not acknowledging him as she
keeps going.

Bobby's eyes throw back his own hostility at her, but
unfortunately she misses it, as he now notices -- across the
street -- a well-kept building with the most modern decor and
signage, reading "McKenna's Realty Co."

He thinks about it, in a quandary.

28   EXT. HIGHWAY/CAR - DAY   28

In a rented convertible, we now see SERGEI racing across the
desert. His jacket off, a man with a mission. He glances at his
watch, eager to get to this "fucking hole in the wall" which is
somewhere on this incomprehensible American map he holds in one
hand.

29   INT. JAKE'S REALTY OFFICE - DAY   29

BOBBY squats, looking at a real estate model of a desert
development. JAKE smiles.

                    JAKE
          What can I do for you, lad?

                    BOBBY
          I was hoping we could talk.

                    JAKE
          Talk? About what?

                    BOBBY
          About things. About your wife.

                    JAKE
          Sweet Grace? What about her?

                    BOBBY
          About what you said this morning.

Jake shakes his head as if he doesn't understand.

                    BOBBY
          You said you had an insurance policy out on
          your wife. Fifty-thousand dollars.

                    JAKE
          I do.

                    BOBBY
          You said you'd cut that up with the man who
          did her in.

                    JAKE
          I did?

                    BOBBY
          Don't play simple with me, Jake. You're a
          betting man. You want me to spell it out
          for you? I'll kill Grace if you cut me in
          on the money.

                    JAKE
          Boy I think this heat's getting to you the way
          you're rambling on.

                    BOBBY
          I'm not rambling.

                                                    (CONTINUED)

                    JAKE
          You're talking like a madman.

                    BOBBY
          Well then, I guess that qualifies me for
          citizenship in this town. You're the one
          brought it up. This morning. In your car.

                    JAKE
          Oh, that was just loose talk. Husband
          gettin' pissed off. I don't want anybody
          dead.

                    BOBBY
          Bullshit. You wanted me to kill her.

                    JAKE
          A man doesn't always mean the things he
          says.

                    BOBBY
          You meant it.

                    JAKE
          What makes you say that?

                    BOBBY
          Because you're a slimy bastard who would
          have his wife killed just to get his hands
          on some money.

                    JAKE
          And what does that make you?

                    BOBBY
          The slimy bastard who's going to do it for
          you... (pause) You're a jealous man Jake.
          If you can't have Grace to yourself...well,
          you're not the sharing kind.

For a moment Jake stares quietly at Bobby.

                    JAKE
          Well, I guess I have what you call a
          love-hate relationship with Grace.

                    BOBBY
          You love her, but you hate her?

                    JAKE
          No, I hate loving her. I hate the kind of
          person she is. I hate having to tolerate
          the little "games" she plays. Like fucking
          half of the town behind my back and
          laughing at me. The bitch. She loved to
          play. She wants me to hit her and when I
          hit her she likes it. She tortures me. But
          she's family. She's my little girl. My
          baby. I couldn't stand to watch her eyes
          roll back in her head as she sucks her last
          breath, or to see her pretty pink brains
          spill from her skull. No. Not me. But you?
          You got the killing in you, boy...How much
          you want?

A pause.

                    BOBBY
          Make it twenty.

                    JAKE (stressed, paces)
          Twenty-thousand? I don't have that kind of
          money. I won't get the insurance until
          months after she's dead. I don't imagine
          you'll want to be stickin' around after
          poor Grace's demise. Twenty-thousand;
          that's more money than I could ever get my
          hands on.

                    BOBBY
          How much could you get?

                    JAKE
          Maybe . . . ten-thousand. And that's a
          maybe.

                    BOBBY
          I need thirteen.

                    JAKE
          That's a bit much.

                    BOBBY
          We're not talking about buying a car Jake.
          We're talking about killing your wife. It's
          thirteen, or it's nothing.

For a moment the two men stand silent. All we hear is the
ticking of a grandfather CLOCK that stands in the corner.

(CONTINUED)

                    JAKE
        You drive a hard bargain, but I had a
        feeling you were my boy when I met you.

                    BOBBY
        I'm not your boy. I don't like you. I got
        no choice but to do business with you.
        Let's just call this a nasty little
        marriage of convenience.

                    JAKE
        Don't say that. I had a marriage of
        convenience with Grace, and look where
        that's lead... Well, looks like we got
        ourselves a contract.

                    BOBBY (sarcastic)
        Do we shake hands?

                    JAKE
        If you can't trust the man you've hired to
        kill your wife . . .? The thing is it's got
        to look like an accident; that's the thing.
        If it doesn't, then it's no good. I won't
        get a dime, and it's my neck that'll be on
        the chopping block while you're living it
        up somewhere.

                    BOBBY
        How do you want it?

                    JAKE
        How the hell should I know? I've never had
        a wife killed before. Jesus Christ! *You*
        want this job, you don't know how to do
        this? I guess I should have hired a
        professional.

                    BOBBY
        You want to do this yourself? I don't have
        to do this, you know.

                    JAKE
        Be quiet, boy. I got to figure this thing.
        I'm thinking. It can't be done at the
        house. It should be...

Jake walks the office thinking.

                    BOBBY
        Come to think of it, how 'bout some money
        upfront?

29   CONTINUED: (4)   29

                    JAKE
          Oh yeah sure. Why don't I buy you a plane
          ticket right out of here while I'm at it. I
          know you...
                    (then)
          This is what you do: Go to the house to
          see her.

                    BOBBY
                    (beat)
          And tell her what?

30   EXT. MCKENNA HOUSE - LATER DAY   30

BOBBY stands on the porch talking to GRACE through the screen of
the front door. The look on his face is sincere. Hers' is
skeptical. We see the action take place as we hear Jake's V.O.:

                    JAKE(V.O.)
          ...I don't know. Tell her you had to see
          her. Tell her you don't care if she's
          married or not, you had to be with her.
          Sweet talk the woman. A young buck like
          you must be good at that. Then . . . maybe
          shift the conversation. Get her thinking
          about that jeep of hers. She loves that
          thing. Maybe the only thing she does love.
          She'll want to take you for a ride.

                    BOBBY
          I know you're not surprised I'm back here,
          cause you can read my mind and all.

She's not surpised.

                    GRACE (seeing his new cut)
          That's some cut. I told you to be more
          careful.

                    BOBBY
          Yeah, well I said I was an idiot. Whatta
          you say we get out of here, take a drive
          somewhere, talk...

                    GRACE
          How do you know he's still not here?

                    BOBBY
          Guys like me take those chances. Let's go.

31   EXT. DESERT - DAY   31

GRACE'S JEEP cuts hard across the desert. Grace has a wild, excited look on her face. BOBBY sits next to her looking somewhat nervous

>   JAKE(V.O.)
>   She'll take you out somewhere in the
>   desert. She loves it out there; ridin'
>   through the red rock and the mesas. So do
>   I. I guess we got that in common. She'll
>   ride you out someplace quiet. Someplace
>   deserted.

>   FADE TO:

32   EXT. DESERT - LATER DAY   32

GRACE has stopped the JEEP on a plateau. BOBBY sits beneath its shade while Grace walks in the sun seemingly unaffected by the heat. VULTURES swoop above.

>   JAKE(V.O.)
>   There won't be anyone for miles around.
>   Just the two of you and some prairie dogs.
>   That's all. You can sweet talk her a
>   little if you like. Makes no difference to
>   me. Just put her at ease, make her feel
>   relaxed -- *then do it.*

JAKE'S V.O. ends. The scene is now synch with real time.

>   BOBBY
>   Are there snakes out here?

>   GRACE
>   They hear you comin'. They won't bother
>   you. Just don't sneak up on 'em.

>   BOBBY
>   Doesn't the isolation bother you?

>   GRACE
>   Yeah, but I like the sun. I grew up on a
>   reservation. The sun, the desert; they
>   like a religion to us. Jake's the same
>   way. He loves the desert. I guess we're
>   alike that way. That's about the only way.

>   BOBBY
>   You love him?

                          GRACE
          No.

                          BOBBY
          Did you ever?

                          GRACE
          Depends on what you call love. I grew up on
          a reservation. A patch of desert in the
          middle of nowhere. That's where they stick
          Indians, Bobby. That's where they leave us
          to die. My brother killed himself when he
          was 19 cause he couldn't take it anymore.
          There's no hope there... Jake was my ticket
          out. Mom and me.

                          BOBBY
          Is that why you're with him?

                          GRACE
          I let him think he was courtin' me, but I
          reeled him in like a fish on a line. I
          wanted him. I wanted what he could give me,
          and I would've done anything to get him. Is
          that love?

                          BOBBY
          I'm guessing no.

                          GRACE
          Yeah, I guess you're right.

                          BOBBY
          I take it things didn't much work out the
          way you planned.

                          GRACE
          I'm still here, aren't I? See this?

          Grace sweeps her hand before her across the expanse of the
          desert. The vultures are very much a part of this landscape.

                          GRACE(CONT)
          All this nothing? It doesn't get to Jake
          like it gets to me. He says he don't mind
          being nothing but a big fish in a small
          pond. More like a little fish in a dried
          up watering hole.

                          BOBBY
          You could leave him.

(CONTINUED)

                          GRACE
          I don't know how.

                          BOBBY
          Walk away.

                          GRACE
          It's not that easy. Maybe you can take
          chances; maybe you can wander around like
          some stray wherever you please. I can't.
          I don't want to be alone. I need to know
          I'm going to be taken care of.

                          BOBBY
          You need a meal ticket is what you mean.
          Some guy you can latch onto just long
          enough for him to get you out of here.

                          GRACE
          Is that so bad? It's not like I wouldn't
          try to make him happy. For awhile anyway.
          I mean, I would . . . do things for him. I
          guess I'm no good that way. I guess I
          tried to sucker you along like that. Do
          you hate me for it? I wouldn't blame you
          if you did. But maybe it's like you said:
          You just got to do whatever it takes to get
          out.

                          BOBBY (soft echo)
          Whatever it takes.

          Grace steps to the edge of the plateau.

                          GRACE
          I wish I was a bird. I know it's stupid.
          Every child says that. When I was growing
          up some of the old ones on the reservation
          believed people could actually change into
          animals. I wish I could.

          We see Bobby behind Grace. He stares at her standing on the
          edge of the plateau. He rises and walks towards her slowly, but
          with deliberation.

                          GRACE(CONT)
          If I was a bird I would fly to Florida; to
          Disney World. I always wanted to go there.
          I'd fly to New York. Maybe. I guess New
          York isn't the best place to be a bird.
          I'd fly to St. Louis, then New Orleans, all
          over Texas. Then I'd fly to California. I
                          (MORE)

                                                      (CONTINUED)

32   CONTINUED: (3)   32

                          GRACE (cont'd)
            guess by then I'd have seen it all and I
            could die.

Bobby now stands a few feet behind Grace. She kicks a rock and watches it sail over the lip of the cliff into the nothingness below.

                         GRACE(CONT)
            They say you don't feel anything. The
            shock kills you before you hit the ground.
            I don't know how they would know that. But
            I heard it's just like flying; straight
            down into the ground. I guess if it
            doesn't hurt it's a beautiful thing.

Bobby tenses himself. Sweat forms on his brow as he stands directly behind Grace with his hands extended before him. They hover just below her shoulder blades ready to push forward. Suddenly Grace wheels. Startled by Bobby she almost falls over the edge. Bobby grabs her, her weight still going back. Grace's life is literally in his hands. She looks down at the ground far below, then up into Bobby's eyes. She shows no fear, but instead wears a curious smirk.

                         GRACE
            Hate's a funny thing. Right now I bet you
            don't know if you want to kill me, or fuck
            me.

Bobby hesitates, then pulls Grace close and kisses her with great ardor on the lips.

33   EXT. APACHE LEAP - DAY   33

On a blanket on the ground, BOBBY and GRACE make love quickly, hotly, her dress pulled up, his pants down. But Grace is troubled and pulls out, further frustrating Bobby.

                         GRACE
            No...Stop! I can't!

Her eyes withdraw into another dimension, as she hikes her dress back up. Bobby comes out of his own head, feels the distance between them.

                         BOBBY
            What's the matter?...Grace?

                         GRACE
             Nothing.

                         BOBBY
             Don't feel like nothing.

He finishes relieving himself behind a tree, puts his pants back
on.

> GRACE
> Get out of town, Bobby, as quick as you
> can.

> BOBBY
> Grace, I've been fucked over too many
> times, by too many women. You're becoming
> the queen of hot and cold.

> GRACE
> You'd never understand.

> BOBBY
> Try me.

> GRACE
> It's just such a mess. With Jake I mean...

> BOBBY
> Nothing I understand better than a mess.

> GRACE (in great tension)
> Jake was with my Mom after my real Dad
> died.

> BOBBY
> You mean the Shaman?

> GRACE
> He _was_ a Shaman...in the mine. We had
> nothin' after he died. Jake took us in,
> gave us a little money. He used to call me
> his "little halfbreed"... He kept Mom on
> the side y'know, cause he was married
> someplace else. He had kids in Phoenix I
> think, no one knew him around here...but
> the thing was...you see...
>> (pause)
> ...he was raping me the whole time...for
> years. He loved to do things to me. Believe
> it or not, he used to say he was in love
> with my ass. Y'ever been in love with a
> woman's ass?

The dominoes are tumbling for Bobby.

> BOBBY
> Yeah.

                        GRACE
            You're sick too...He loved to do things to
            me. Control me. My Mom...it tore her up
            cause she couldn't do nothing about it. She
            become alcoholic...and the funny thing is--
            I liked it. I liked being controlled by
            Jake. The truth was as far out and crazy as
            he got, I wanted *more*. I wanted to go all
            the way. Woman say they don't want to be
            taken like, *really taken* -- that's bullshit
            -- they do. The first time he finished with
            me, he said I was a woman now. I was 14.
            Then he started crying like a baby...wanted
            me to hold him. It's a strange feeling to
            hate someone so much for so many years, but
            still want to hold him, comfort him... They
            found my Mom right down there (points) at
            the bottom of Apache Leap. She had cactus
            needles stuck all over her body and
            Virgil...Sheriff Potter said she was drunk
            and went insane. But I'll never believe she
            ran off that cliff by accident. She was
            born on this earth and she loved it. She
            was like me. She just wanted to fly away.

Bobby is quietly stunned. A whole world has opened up to him;
and he isn't sure yet where the story ends. There is some force
at work here, beyond his control.

                        GRACE
            After he got his divorce, he forced me to
            marry him...but when I saw her body, I
            swore to her on my soul that some day I'd
            get Jake for what he did to her...

                        BOBBY
            I'm sorry...

                        GRACE
            Yeah. What do you want. Life, right?
            (shrugs, stoic) Have you ever been to
            California?

                        BOBBY
            Yeah.

                        GRACE (as if a dream)
            Is it far from here?

                        BOBBY
            Oh yeah. It's far, it's another world.

                                                    (CONTINUED)

>   GRACE
>   Is it pretty?

>   BOBBY
>   Oh yeah. It's beautiful, beautiful beaches.
>   Blue water and clear skies as far as you
>   can see.

>   GRACE (like a little girl)
>   Would you take me with you?

>   BOBBY (pause)
>   I wish I could, Grace.

>   GRACE
>   Please. I won't hang on you. As soon as we
>   get there you can dump me. I don't care. I
>   just want to get out of here.

>   BOBBY
>   Honey, baby, I *can't*. I can't even get out
>   of here *myself*. Believe it or not, I need a
>   lousy hundred and fifty bucks to get my car
>   back from that crazy mechanic...

>   GRACE
>   Darrell? You know he and Jake are...

>   BOBBY
>   You don't have any money put away, do you?

>   GRACE
>   Jake never gives me more'n twenty bucks at
>   a time, like a bird in a cage, he don't
>   want me goin' anywhere...

>   BOBBY
>   ...you could get some money. I'll get you
>   out of here.

She looks at him.

>   GRACE
>   There's money. A lot.

The words hang there, thick between them.

>   BOBBY
>   Where?

33   CONTINUED: (4)   33

> GRACE
> Jake hides it. In a safe. In the floor. In the bedroom. He counts it. He loves to sit there and count it.

> BOBBY
> What do you mean?

> GRACE
> At night. He just sits there and laughs and talks to himself and counts it. I heard him. My Mom told me he had a hunnert thousand dollars there. Maybe more.

Bobby's eyes widen in hope.

> BOBBY
> In *cash*?

> GRACE
> Oh yeah. There's nothing else with Jake. He don't trust banks. He keeps the money in the floor right under the bed. He loves it so much, he wouldn't think of spending any of it on me. I never seen it but I know he's got more than a hunnert thousand at least...

> BOBBY
> One-hundred-thousand!? That son-of-a-bitch.

> GRACE (puzzled)
> What do you mean?

> BOBBY (ignoring her)
> If it's in a safe we'd have to get the combination--

> GRACE
> It takes a key. He keeps it on himself all the time. I mean *all the time*. It scratches up against me when we do it.

> BOBBY
> If the key's on him, how do we get the key?

> GRACE
> Kill him.

Spoken almost innocently, it hangs there between them. A silence.

(CONTINUED)

                              BOBBY
                    I can't kill, Grace. I can't kill anybody.

                              GRACE
                    It's not like he's a young man, Bobby. He's
                    had time to live. It'd be quick. I mean, he
                    wouldn't even have to *feel* it...
                        (seductively) I mean, sometime in the
                    middle of the night, when it's quiet...when
                    he's asleep, you could just come up behind
                    him when he's pounding on me and...

Grace lays her hands on Bobby, starting to caress him. He
bristles and freezes in fear and disgust.

                              BOBBY
                    Shit! Listen to you... Are you crazy,
                    Grace?

He abruptly pulls away.

                              BOBBY
                    Jesus Christ! I think this place is making
                    me crazy. I was crazy to come back here and
                    see you. I'm crazy for listening to anyone
                    in this town, and I'd sure as hell be crazy
                    if I spent another minute with you.

Grace rises, covering her nakedness, shooting a hand to his
face, like she did when she read his fortune.

                              GRACE
                    But it's in you, Bobby. I see it. I see
                    Death. It's in your heart. Let it out for
                    me. Let it out...

He's mesmerized. Then:

                              GRACE
                    Do it for me, Bobby, you'll never regret
                    it. I promise you. I'll do anything for
                    you. *Anything.*

Bobby pauses, terribly torn.

                              BOBBY
                    I...take me back to town...

He turns away, towards the jeep. Grace has a tone of desperation
in her voice.

                                                    (CONTINUED)

CONTINUED: (6)

                              GRACE
                    You need the money, Bobby. It's a lot more
                    than $100,000. A lot more. How are you
                    going to get out of here? You need the
                    money. Whatever it takes, Bobby, remember?

Bobby walks past the jeep, on his way back to town alone.

                              GRACE
                    Where you going? I'll give you the
                    ride...Come back! Bobby? It's three miles.

Bobby does't look back. Her eyes drift backwards into her
solitude.

                              GRACE (to herself)
                    Bobby?...Whatever it takes.

34   EXT. DESERT/ALONG THE ROAD - LATER DAY   34

BOBBY walks through the desert parallel to the road, still in a
rage. Desert insects produce a cacophony of drones, buzzes, and
clicks. A rattlesnake darts off a rock into the brush. A VOICE
whispers to him.

                              JAKE (V.O.)
                    You've got the killing in you, boy.

Bobby turns and looks around. Just desert. He continues.

                              JAKE (V.O.)
                    Next time you'll do just fine.

                              BOBBY
                    No!

The screen burns a bright white.

35   EXT. STREET CORNER - DAY   35

In a new spot, further down the street from where he was first
seen, the old, BLIND MAN sits with his dead DOG, speaking as if
into camera, sipping on a Dr. Pepper.

                              BLIND MAN
                    It's the desert that makes you crazy. The
                    loneliness out here. Nobody to talk to.
                    People on the run. Trailer parks. White
                    trash. I seen some peculiar things on a hot
                    day. I seen a scorpion sting itself to
                    death. It just keeps driving its tail into
                    its body again and again. A little killer
                              (MORE)

35   CONTINUED: 35

> BLIND MAN (cont'd)
> killing itself. Seen a coyote kill itself
> too. Just kept on biting and tearing at
> its own legs. Near tore one clean off
> before it bled to death. And what a white
> man'll do when it's freezing one moment,
> hot as hell the next. A man could get
> hisself killed just for rubbing shoulders
> with another (smacking his lips) kiss kissy
> kiss. Nice pussy y'see, see it coming. I
> don't know what it is about the desert. I
> figger it's sort of like putting a kettle
> of water over a fire. People is mostly
> water. We boil when it's hot. 'Cept when
> we boil the water's got no place to go. It
> just churns inside of us until we can cool
> off. If it's not too late.

BOBBY is now revealed standing next to the blind man, and we
realize the blind man has been talking to him all along. Bobby
sips a Dr. Pepper as well.

> BOBBY
> You sure seen a lot for a blind man.

> BLIND MAN
> Just 'cause I ain't got eyes doesn't mean I
> can't see.

> BOBBY
> That a fact?

Bobby noticing now all the little NEWSPAPER CLIPPINGS that the
Blind Man keeps around him in a sort of inchoate stall.

> BLIND MAN
> I can see just fine. For example: You're
> a young man who thinks he's got someplace
> to be.

A POLICE RADIO crackles, Bobby tensing.

> BOBBY
> Maybe I do.

> BLIND MAN
> Or maybe you just think you do. Just
> another small town. One guy chasing you.
> You go big town. Just gonna have four guys
> after you instead. Kiss kissy kiss. It gets
> down to one thing -- are you a human being
> or are you one of those hungry ghosts out
> there never satisfied with nothing? Cause
> you gotta remember you can run just as far
> (MORE)

(CONTINUED)

35   CONTINUED: (2)   35

                          BLIND MAN (cont'd)
as you can, but wherever you go, that's
where you gonna be.

                        BOBBY
I think I've heard that before.

                      BLIND MAN
What do you want for free?

                        BOBBY
You sure got a lot of philosophy, old man.

                      BLIND MAN
Seems like I do but only cause end of the
day we're all eyes in the same head. And
everything is everything.

                        BOBBY
What?

                      BLIND MAN
...And everything is nothing too.

                      BOBBY (shakes his head)
Maybe one day I'll get to sit on a corner
and spout wise.

                      BLIND MAN
Think you'll live that long?

Bobby is clearly unnerved by this. Suddenly the blind man
stands, pissed and powerful, sniffing the air with the police
radio in it.

As SHERIFF POTTER cruises by, glancing at Bobby shrinking. The
car goes on up the street.

                      BLIND MAN
Cocksucker motherfucker! Cops. I hear you.
Always sneaking around. Thinks I can't see
him. Well he's right. Motherfucker. But
that ain't mean I don't know what's going
on around here. They're all cursed. Yes
sir.

                        BOBBY
Who's cursed?

                      BLIND MAN
All them miners last century. Hungry
ghosts, killed off all the Indians. Up at
the mine. Earth ran red with blood, think
I'm fooling around here. White sky was on
fire. Grown men cried like babies. I saw a
                      (MORE)

                                                 (CONTINUED)

35   CONTINUED: (3)   35

                              BLIND MAN (cont'd)
              flash, then darkness descended upon me.
              They put me in the joint. Took my eyes. I
              cursed them. White people can't seem to
              stay away from Indians (grabs his bandaged
              hand, smelling the blood). You gotta watch
              where ya put your fingers. Pussy pussy
              pussy, Indian pussy.

    It sounds demented. Bobby, checking him out to see if he's
    really blind, walks quietly around him during this monologue and
    peeks over his glasses trying to see the blind man's real eyes.
    Although he thinks the Blind Man thinks he's on the other side
    of him, the Blind Man fools him by suddenly swivelling around
    and cranking a gob of spit into Bobby's face as if Bobby were on
    the other side.

    Bobby, pissed, wipes the spittle from his face.

                              BLIND MAN (finishing)
              ...but they gotta know you don't fuck
              around with Indians.

                              BOBBY
              I thought you said you lost your eyes in
              the war?

                              BLIND MAN
              So now you're going to tell me where I lost
              my eyes. You don't think I know where I
              lost my eyes? I was there when I lost them.
              I lost them in the war. The war in the
              joint. There's always wars in the joint.
              Cause I was a code talker in the joint and
              in the war too. (sniffs) Mmmm, nothing like
              the smell of a naked lady. Be careful, boy.

                              BOBBY
              Musta been some bad ass nuclear tests here
              in the 50's. This town's all inbreeding.

                              BLIND MAN
              Well, people gotta get by somehow. That's
              the curse. The mines done it. All that
              uranium, plutonium, fuffonium, fuckononium,
              assononium, all that "om"! Everybody's got
              a mother. You don't rip up your mother. You
              don't rip up the Earth and take everything
              out. It's like the Cracker Jack box says,
              "the more you eat, the more you
              want...."...

                              BOBBY
              I got things to do.

                                                    (CONTINUED)

35   CONTINUED: (4)   35

                         BLIND MAN (offended)
              Oh well, go do 'em. You don't see me
              stopping you...

Bobby starts to walk away. The Blind Man rattles his tin cup.

                         BLIND MAN
              ...But ain't you got a little something for
              the infirm?

                         BOBBY
              I'm a little short Pops. I'll catch you
              next time.

                         BLIND MAN
              Your lies are old, but you tell 'em well.

36   EXT. STREET - DAY   36

BOBBY, depressed, is heading towards Harlin's gas station,
passing JENNY sitting on a corner drinking a soda, almost as if
waiting for him. She runs to him, and follows him, as somewhere
a POLICE RADIO crackles and buzzes.

                         JENNY
              Hey mister. Mister, I just... I just wanted
              to thank you.

                         BOBBY
              For what?

                         JENNY
              For defending my honor this afternoon.

                         BOBBY
              I hate to bust your bubble honey, but I
              wasn't defending you.

                         JENNY
              But you was going to fight for me.

                         BOBBY
              I wasn't going to fight for you. I was
              just going to beat the shit out of your
              boyfriend.

                         JENNY
              He's not my boyfriend. I mean, I let him
              take me out and stuff, but I ain't spoken
              for. Not yet that is.

                                    BOBBY
          Get it through your head, little girl; I'm
          not going for you. If this Toby likes you,
          then if I were you I'd marry him. You're
          not going to get much better in this town.

                                    JENNY
          That's what I thought until you came riding
          in. I saw your car over at the gas
          station. It's a cool car. Want to take me
          for a ride? Desert's kind of lonely this
          time of day.

                                    BOBBY
          How old are you?

                                    JENNY
                    (beat)
          Eighteen... Well, I'm gonna be eighteen in
          two years, but that don't mean you can't
          take me for a ride if you want.

                                    BOBBY
          No, I don't want to take you for a ride.
          What I want is for . . . Hey, you don't
          think you can get $150 from your parents,
          could you?

From OFF CAMERA we hear Toby.

                                    TOBY(O.C.)
          Mister!

                                    BOBBY
          Oh, shit!

Toby moves menacingly up the street towards Bobby.

                                    TOBY
          That's right, Mister. You better be
          afraid. I told you it wasn't over, but you
          didn't listen. Now I find you sneakin'
          around with my girl behind my back.

                                    BOBBY
          I wasn't sneaking around with your girl.
          Would you please tell him?

                                    JENNY
          You're too late, Toby. We're going to get
          in his fancy car and ride off and leave you
          behind.

                                                      (CONTINUED)

                    BOBBY
        What the hell are you talking about?

                    JENNY
        What's your name anyway?

                    TOBY
        Oh, that tears it, Mister. I'm gonna bust
        you up but good. I'm gonna bust you into a
        million pieces and then . . . and then bust
        those pieces up, and then . . . and then
        spread them all around. That's what I'm
        gonna do. You don't know what you're
        dealing with, Mister. I'm crazy. I'm
        psycho crazy.

                    BOBBY
        Yeah, I know. You're TNT. Just like
        dynamite. When you go off somebody gets
        hurt. (at his wit's end) All right. Let's
        do this.

                    JENNY
        Toby Tucker, it don't matter to me if you
        beat him all up and knock out all his teeth
        and he's just drooling and bleeding all
        over hisself, 'cause we love each other and
        we gonna run off, and I'm gonna have his
        love child.

                    BOBBY
        Will you shut up!

                    TOBY
        You gonna pay for that, Mister.

Toby and Bobby square off, sizing each other up and preparing
for a violent confrontation. Just as the two are about to clash
we hear the voice of SHERIFF POTTER from OFF CAMERA.

                    SHERIFF(O.C.)
        Toby!

The two men freeze in their tracks, as Potter drives up fast.

                    TOBY
        Hey, Sheriff Potter.

                    SHERIFF (tough)
        Toby, I just come from your mother's place.
        She's worried sick about you. She says she
        ain't seen you since this morning.

                                                    (CONTINUED)

                         TOBY
              That ain't true, Sheriff. I was home for
              lunch.

                         SHERIFF
              Boy, I'm not trying to hear nothing from
              you except that you're heading home. Now
              run along.

                         TOBY
              Yes, sir. Come on, Jenny.

                         JENNY
              I want to stay.

                         TOBY
              I said come on!

Toby grabs Jenny by the wrist and literally pulls her along. As
she goes she yells back to Bobby.

                         JENNY
              Bye, Mister. Don't go nowhere without me.
              I wanna have your love child.

Toby points a vicious finger at Bobby.

                         TOBY
              Next time, Mister. Next time.

Toby and Jenny exit leaving Bobby and the Sheriff alone. Bobby
would also like to exit fast.

                         SHERIFF
              Where ya goin'?

                         BOBBY
              Harlin's.

                         SHERIFF
              Get in.

Bobby has no choice. He gets in.

                         SHERIFF
              Seen you popping up a little bit of
              everywhere today. You're not planning on
              staying are you?

                         BOBBY
              No, sir. I'm not going to be around long if
              that's what you're worried about.

                                                    (CONTINUED)

                    SHERIFF
          That's a nasty cut you got there.

                    BOBBY
          Yeah, fell down and hit a rock. Not as bad
          as it looks.

                    SHERIFF
          There was a young fellow over at Jamilla's
          today when it got hit. Way she tells it he
          got whacked around good by one of the
          robbers.

                    BOBBY
          Sounds like it. I wish I could help
          Sheriff, but I just want to get my car and
          get on the road.

JAKE drives up in his GOLD CADDY. His windows whirr down.

                    JAKE
          Everything all right, Virgil?

He eyes Bobby.

                    SHERIFF (a little nervous)
          Just fine, Jake. Where you going?

                    JAKE
          I was just up at Darrell's. How's the wife?
          That little eskimo baby walkin' yet?

                    SHERIFF
          Oh just fine.

                    JAKE
          You haven't seen Grace around, have you?
          I'm looking for her.

                    SHERIFF
          No. But if I do, I'll tell her you're
          looking for her, Jake.

                    JAKE (looking at Bobby)
          Whatcha got there, some trash?

He drives off. The Sheriff drives on.

                    SHERIFF
          Peculiar, how things happen. A man's car
          breaks down. There's a hold up. People die
          and all that money -- and now old Jake out
                    (MORE)

                                        (CONTINUED)

36 CONTINUED: (5)   36

                              SHERIFF (cont'd)
                    looking for his young wife. And then *you*
                    show up...

The Sheriff looks right through Bobby, who knows this is more
than a conversation. He pulls up to Harlin's garage. Bobby gets
out.

                              SHERIFF
                    Time's running out, son. I'll be seeing you
                    in the morning...

With this thinly veiled threat, the Sheriff drives on. As Bobby
watches, feeling the pressure to get out now while he can.

37 EXT. HARLIN'S GARAGE - LATER DAY   37

DARRELL is cleaning his tools. Bobby's MUSTANG sits prominently
in the car bay, washed and gleaming, as BOBBY walks up.

                              DARRELL
                    Hey there. I was beginnin' to think you
                    wasn't comin' back... You don't look so
                    good.

                              BOBBY
                    Yeah, well, I've been around the bend a
                    bit.

                              DARRELL
                    One of those days you feel like you been
                    runnin' in circles and you ain't no closer
                    to where you tryin' to get than when you
                    started?

                              BOBBY
                    You've been there?

                              DARRELL
                    Hell, I've had days I would gladly trade
                    with a whippin' dog. Ain't much you can do
                    when you feel like that 'cept tough it out.

                              BOBBY
                    You believe that?

                              DARRELL
                    You think bad, and bad is what you get.

                              BOBBY
                    That's a good piece of advice, Darrell.

                              DARRELL
                    No charge.

                                                            (CONTINUED)

                    BOBBY
          Listen, Darrell, about that hundred-fifty
          bucks for the car, as soon as I get where
          I'm going I swear I'll--

                    DARRELL
          Two-hundred.

                    BOBBY
          What?

                    DARRELL
          It's going to cost you two-hundred dollars.

                    BOBBY
          You said this morning the hose was going to
          run me one-fifty.

                    DARRELL
          Yep. For the hose. But while you was gone
          I replaced a gasket. That's going to run
          you another fifty.

                    BOBBY
          I didn't tell you to replace any gasket.

                    DARRELL
          Yeah, but it was shot.

                    BOBBY
          I don't give a fuck! I didn't tell you to
          do it! You can't just do unauthorized
          work.

                    DARRELL
          Well, now, you just know all there is about
          bein' a mechanic, don't you? Didn't you
          read the sign.

                    BOBBY
          What sign?

                    DARRELL
          The goddamn sign on the wall. I can't do
          unauthorized work? What am I suppose to
          do? Just let you ride out of here with a
          bad gasket. Then you get in an accident
          and get killed. Or worse. Who they gonna
          blame then? They gonna blame me, and there
          goes my reputation.

                              BOBBY
          What reputation? You're nothing but an
          ignorant, inbred, tumbleweed hick.

                              DARRELL
          Is that an insult? Are you insulting me.

                              BOBBY
          Listen you stupid fuck, I want my car.

                              DARRELL
          Listen to me you sorry sonufabitch. You owe
          me money, and this car ain't going nowheres
          until I get it. And if you take another
          five hours I'll find another fifty dollars
          worth of work to do on it. Is that clear?
          Now get out of here 'fore I call the
          Sheriff, who knows me.

Bobby is in a rage. He turns to leave and walks a few paces.
He sees a WRENCH lying on a table. For a second his mind reels,
then he snatches up the wrench and turns ready to smash it down
on Darrell's head. He stops cold. Because ol' Darrell holds a
CROWBAR in a batter's stance ready to smash it into the Mustang.

                              DARRELL
          You want to play, Mister? I'll play with
          you. You want to smash something? So do
          I.

Darrell pulls back the crowbar, ready to swing.

                              BOBBY
          No! Okay! Okay!

                              DARRELL
          What's the matter? The fight gone out of
          you? I'm just gonna smash a headlight.
          Maybe two.

                              BOBBY (pleading, almost crying)
          Please, just leave the car alone!

                              DARRELL
          Mister, you already pissed me off but good.

Darrell lays the tip of the crowbar on the hood of the car, and
drags the tip of the bar across the hood leaving a long scratch.

                              BOBBY (about to lose it)
          Goddamn you! You son of a bitch!

                                                    (CONTINUED)

37   CONTINUED: (3)   37

                              DARRELL
                    There you go, sweet talking me again.

Darrell begins to laugh. Bobby, desperate, looks to the trunk,
thinking of his gun in there.

His POV -- the trunk. A FLASHBACK of the GUN goes through his
mind.

                              BOBBY
                    Look, Harlin.

                              DARRELL
                    Darrell.

                              BOBBY
                    Darrell. I'll get you your money. I just
                    have to get something out of the trunk.

Using his TRUNK KEY, he tries to open it but realizes the lock
has been changed.

                              BOBBY
                    What the fuck did you do to my trunk?

                              DARRELL
                    Well, that key's not gonna work. I had to
                    pop the lock. You didn't leave me the trunk
                    key.

                              BOBBY
                    And you had to go into the trunk, didn't
                    you?

                              DARRELL
                    When I work on a car, I work on a car.

                              BOBBY (snaps)
                    You motherfucker! (etc.)

                              DARRELL
                    You can't help yourself, can you mister?
                    You're out of control.

Darrell starts to laugh. It is a repetitive, almost demonic
laugh that grows louder as the camera slowly dollies in on
Bobby's anguished face.

38   EXT. STREET - DAY   38

As BOBBY steps out into the glaring sun, he notices down at the
other end of the town, GRACE'S JEEP parked right outside the
SHERIFF'S OFFICE, empty.

                                                          (CONTINUED)

38   CONTINUED: 38

        Presently, GRACE and the SHERIFF walk out talking, and she gets
        in, says a few last words and drives away.

        Bobby backs around a corner into a sidestreet. Is she selling
        him out? He's very confused, turbulent.

39   INT. BUS DEPOT - LATER DAY   39

        BOBBY enters the BUS DEPOT. The interior is poorly lit. There
        are a few benches for people to wait on, but they sit empty.
        Old, faded travel posters hang on the wall. A bored FEMALE
        CLERK is behind the counter.

                          BOBBY
                I need a ticket.

                          CLERK
                Where to?

                          BOBBY
                Out of here.

                          CLERK
                But, in particular?

                          BOBBY
                I . . . Mexico. You got a bus that goes to
                Mexico? That's where I have to go.

                          CLERK
                Mexico is a large country. Where in Mexico
                would you like--

                          BOBBY
                I don't care, just get me there.

        The clerk is a little put off by Bobby. He seems delirious. She
        goes through her schedule looking for a bus.

                          CLERK
                How about Cuidad Juarez? You could take a
                local, arrives in two hours, and transfer
                in Albuquerque. It'll get you across the
                border.

                          BOBBY
                How much?

                          CLERK
                One way, or round trip?

                          BOBBY
                One way.

                                                        (CONTINUED)

CONTINUED:

> CLERK
> 30.55. Twenty more will get you back.

Bobby counts his money.

> BOBBY
> Twenty-seven, fifty. That's all I got.

> CLERK
> The ticket is 30.55.

> BOBBY (rifling his pockets)
> I bought a beer. That was a dollar
> something. Then I gave that girl 25 cents
> for the juke box. And the blind man...the
> soda...I...I'd have 30 if...if...

> CLERK
> I'm sorry, sir. It's $30.55 for the
> ticket.

> BOBBY (to himself)
> Yeah. Just a little short. Figures. I
> just wanted to get out, that's all.

Bobby starts to walk away. Suddenly he turns, runs back at the
clerk, proffers his money, half-crazed, near tears.

> BOBBY
> Please, ma'am, you don't understand! I *have*
> to get out of here. They're going to come
> looking for me. *They're going to kill me*.
> If I can't get this ticket then I'm going
> to have to do things to get out of here.
> *You know what I mean!* I don't want to hurt
> anybody, I just want to leave. *Please*. I
> can't...I can't.

He's so desperate and in her frightened but neutral expression,
Bobby experiences the only compassion he ever finds in this
whole town.

> CLERK
> Okay, I'll give you the ticket, sir,
> but...just...just, please calm down,
> please!

Her sane tone reminds Bobby of how far down he's come. He
shrinks, suddenly ashamed of himself. She takes the cash on the
counter, hands him a ticket.

39   CONTINUED: (2)   39

                          CLERK
               Keep your change. Bus three-twenty-three.
               Leaves at seven fifty two, tonight.

                          BOBBY
               I'm sorry. It's just . . . you know . . .

She nods, puts a "closed" sign in the ticket window, disappears.

40   EXT. BUS DEPOT - LATE DAY   40

We hear the crackle of the same POLICE RADIO again, OFF CAMERA.
as BOBBY walks out of the depot, ticket preciously held in his
hand, and suddenly reels as he sees SERGEI, about a 100 yards
down the main stretch, slowly rolling into town in his
convertible, looking for guess who.

                          BOBBY
               Holy shit!

41   INT. SERGEI'S CAR - SIMULTANEOUS   41

BOBBY turns away, but not fast enough. SERGEI spots him, hits
the pedal.

                          SERGEI
               Got you, shitface! Bobby Cooper. Bobby
               Cooper...

42   EXT. MAIN STREET - SIMULTANEOUS   42

Bobby, ducking around a corner, hears the brief "Whoop" of the
sheriff's POLICE SIREN. He glances back.

His POV - sure enough, the SHERIFF'S having a field day. He's
just pulled SERGEI over. At this distance, we catch snippets of
conversation as the Sheriff ambles from his car, checking
Sergei's out-of-state plates.

                          SHERIFF
               Where's the fire sweetheart? Don't know how
               they work things in Nevada, but we got
               speed limits in this state.

                          SERGEI
               Vat? I am going 5 miles an hour! I am
               looking town. I not even moving.

We pop in closer to their conversation -- BOBBY relishing this
in his mind's eye. Sergei is constantly looking off to where he
last saw Bobby. But the Sheriff, strangely, pays no attention to
these looks.

                                                    (CONTINUED)

42   CONTINUED:

                    SHERIFF
          Whoa, what kind of accent you got there?
          You one of them Russians?

                    SERGEI
          I am Russian, da! I am also *rich* Russian,
          da? Maybe we work something out, my friend
          Sheriff?

                    SHERIFF
          What? You trying to bribe me, mister? Just
          cause you Russians ain't commies anymore,
          don't think money can buy everything...

Down the street, SHERIFF POTTER is holding up a concealed GUN.

                    SHERIFF
          What's that? (He grabs the gun)
          ..."concealed" is a definite no no in this
          town, Ivan. You know anything about
          Jamilla's grocery store?

                    SERGEI
          What fuckin grocery store, you fucking
          shithead idiot! You call yourself a
          police...

SERGEI looking in Bobby's direction.

                    SHERIFF
          Get out of the car, spread them. You can
          jawbone all you want or you have the right
          to *shut the fuck up!* You commie
          motherfucker. Either way you're goin' to
          the can.

                    SERGEI
          I want my lawyer!

Sheriff cuffs Sergei and sticks him in the police car.

Bobby can't help smiling as he turns away to the SODA MACHINE
seen in an earlier scene.

He comes up with the change the bus clerk left him and, dying
for a drink in this heat, inserts the coin. Though still under
considerable pressure from all sides, this lucky break with
Sergei seems like it might be the beginning of something new
today -- some luck.

The icy cold soda bottle shoots out. Bobby raises it to his
lips, about to taste it, about to relax for once. Violently it
explodes out of his hands as he doubles over in blinding pain

                                              (CONTINUED)

from a KIDNEY PUNCH. He stumbles forward into the soda machine,
gasping. The legs of his assailant are close on him, but the
face is unseen.

Bobby doubles his agony as his bandaged left stump takes the
brunt of the blow into the machine, re-opening the wound. Blood
starts to seep through the bandage.

                    BOBBY
          Ow!

Bobby crumples to the ground as TOBY now towers over him with
his fists curled and a snarl on his lips.

                    TOBY
          Get up, Mister! Don't ever let it be said
          Toby Tucker beat the living shit out of
          someone without giving them a fair chance.

                    BOBBY (gasping)
          What the hell are you doing? You fucking
          psycho!

                    TOBY
          I'm doing what any man would do if he'd
          been offended. I'm stompin' your ass.

                    BOBBY
          You idiot! You don't even know what you're
          fighting over!

                    TOBY
          My honor, that's what I'm fighting over.
          Now get up off the ground, or do I have to
          whoop you where you lie?

JENNY comes running up the street.

                    JENNY
          Toby! Toby Tucker, leave him alone!

                    TOBY
          You stay away, Jenny. I aim to mess him
          up, and that ain't a thing for a woman to
          see.

Jenny runs to Bobby and cuddles him where he lays.

                    JENNY
          Don't be afraid of him none. I don't care
          what he does to you, we can still be
          together.

                                        (CONTINUED)

CONTINUED: (3)

                              BOBBY
                    Get away from me!

Bobby sees his bus ticket on the ground. He grabs for it, but
Toby beats him to it.

                              TOBY
                    Now, what's this?

                              BOBBY
                    Give it to me!

                              TOBY
                    Mexico? You going to Mexico?

                              BOBBY
                    I'm leaving. You never have to see me
                    again. Just please, give me the ticket!

                              TOBY
                    This means something to you? Jenny means
                    something to me.

Toby sticks the ticket in his mouth and chews it up whole.

                              BOBBY
                    Nooo!

                              TOBY (between bites)
                    I'm gonna beat you so bad you gonna be
                    eatin' nothing but soup the rest of your
                    days. Rain dogs is gonna be prettier than
                    you when I'm done. I'm gonna mess you up
                    so bad you gonna make your own momma sick.
                    I'm gonna . . .

Toby's words drift to Bobby from a million miles away. The
world around him is like a dream, or a nightmare. A primal rage
wells inside of Bobby that rises up in a howl as he swings the
soda bottle up out of nowhere across Toby's head, smashing him
backwards. Then he lands blow after blow with his right hand on
the boy's face and head.

Jenny screams:

                              JENNY
                    Stop it! You're killing him!

Jenny grabs Bobby's arm, literally hanging all her weight on it,
stopping him from striking Toby again.

                              JENNY
                    You're killing him! Toby!? Toby!?

42   CONTINUED: (4)   42

Jenny sinks to the ground and cuddles Toby. Bobby stands. He
looks at Toby, then at his bloodied knuckles in disbelief. His
bandage is soaked with his own blood, but his adrenaline numbs
the pain.

                    JENNY
          You killed him! You killed him!

She wails in the background as he backs away, around the corner,
into Main Street, crossing to where the PHONE BOOTH is.

43   EXT. PHONE BOOTH - LATE DAY   43

BOBBY is on the phone.

                    BOBBY
          Hello, Grace? It's Bobby.

                                                    INTERCUTS TO:

44   INT. MCKENNA HOUSE - SIMULTANEOUS   44

GRACE, in the kitchen, is also on the phone.

                    GRACE (coolly)
          I thought you'd be on your way to Vegas by
          now. Is there something you wanted?

                    BOBBY
          I wanted to talk.

                    GRACE(V.O.)
          I don't think we have anything to talk
          about.

                    BOBBY
          What about us?

                    GRACE
          There is no us, remember?

                    BOBBY
          Except I can't get you out of my head,
          Grace.
                    (beat)

          I've thought about you every second since I
          left. I can still taste you on my lips.

                    GRACE
          Stop it.

> BOBBY (V.O.)
> Why? Am I making you hot, or does the
> truth scare you?

> GRACE
> Because I know you're full of shit.

> BOBBY
> I mean it, Grace. I'm getting out of here,
> and I want to take you with me.

> GRACE (V.O.)
> I thought you couldn't get your car.

> BOBBY
> I could if I had Jake's money.

> GRACE (V.O.)
> Is that what changed your mind? The money?

> BOBBY
> I don't give a damn about the money. I
> want you, and I want to get us out of this
> shithole. There's only one way to do that.

Pause.

> GRACE
> Are you sure?... About me, I mean?

> BOBBY
> I came back for you; this morning I came
> back. Before I even knew about the money.
> You're what I want.
>   (then)
> The only reason I stormed off is because
> you spooked me talking about Jake. But
> I've had nothing but time to think about
> it. It keeps coming back to you and me and
> us getting the hell out of here. But we've
> got to get the money, baby. We get the
> money, I get the car, then we get the hell
> out.

> GRACE
> You said you couldn't kill anybody.

> BOBBY
> We don't have to kill him. Just knock him
> out and tie him up 'till we get away.
>   (beat)
> It was your idea, remember? I'm doing this
>   (MORE)

44   CONTINUED: (2)   44

> BOBBY (cont'd)
> for you. I'm doing this so you can
> fly...fly like a bird.

Grace bites at a nail and fidgets, but says nothing.

> BOBBY (V.O.)
> Grace . . . Grace?

> GRACE
> After dark. I'll leave the back door
> unlocked.

She quickly hangs up the phone.

Bobby also hangs up the phone, an unreadable expression on his
face.

45   INT. MCKENNA LIVING ROOM - LATE DAY   45

JAKE sits in an easy chair reading a paper. Puffs of smoke from
his pipe rise from behind the paper and hang like a cloud over
his head. GRACE stands in the doorway, body stiff and arms
crossed, staring at him.

> JAKE
> Who was on the phone?

> GRACE
> Wrong number.

> JAKE
> You spent a long time talking for a wrong
> number. But then you make friends so
> easily. Don't you, Grace?

Grace has no answer for that, so she says nothing. A long
moment passes, then:

> GRACE
> I put up new drapes, Jake.

> JAKE
> I know. I was here when your apprentice
> was helping you. Remember?

> GRACE
> You never said anything. About the drapes.

> JAKE
> They look nice.

> GRACE
> You haven't even looked at them once.

(CONTINUED)

45   CONTINUED: 45

Jake lowers the paper, looks at the drapes.

                        JAKE
                They look nice.

                        GRACE
                I picked them out for you, Jake. I thought
                you would like the colors.

                        JAKE (softly, admiring)
                You look just like your mama when you move
                like that against the light.

Grace stares at the CHAIN now visible around Jake's neck that
disappears under his shirt. She knows that hidden there is a
key, and she fixes on it intently.

                        JAKE
                What the hell you looking at, girl?

                        GRACE
                Nothing, Jake. Absolutely nothing.

46   EXT. DESERT - EVENING   46

The SUN is setting. It strikes the horizon sending a ripple of
golden light through the sky.

47   EXT. PORCH OF HOUSE - EVENING   47

A MAN dances in the evening light with a small child in his
arms.

48   EXT. CORNER OF HOUSE - EVENING   48

A DOG and CAT huddle together in sleep.

49   EXT. POLICE STATION -- EVENING   49

SHERIFF VIRGIL POTTER is tossing horseshoes with his DEPUTIES.

50   EXT. MCKENNA HOUSE - DAY   50

GRACE watches the sun going down outside her house, cradling
herself in her arms. A desert wind gently caresses her.

51   EXT. STREET CORNER - NIGHT   51

The BLIND MAN, along with his dead DOG, sits on the side of the
street.

51   CONTINUED: 51

> BLIND MAN
> Well, that's it. Sun's going down. People
> go home, trade stories over dinner.
> They'll talk about the day, about the heat,
> laugh about something crazy it made them
> do. They'll kiss, sleep a few hours, then
> do it all over again.

BOBBY now appears next to the blind man holding two Dr. Peppers.
He hands one to the blind man, takes a sip of the other one, and
offers him his own change.

> BOBBY
> The day wasn't so bad. We all got through
> it all right.

> BLIND MAN (giving back the change)
> Keep it.

There's a suggestion of cockiness in Bobby, feeling his luck
coming back with the night. His humour is enhanced by his POV
down the street:

As DARRELL, with his dilapidated truck, readies SERGEI'S
convertible for towing.

> BLIND MAN (OVER)
> Ain't over yet. Night is part of day;
> separate, but equal. Night is when you let
> your guard down; when you see things in the
> shadows and hear things in the dark.

> BOBBY
> Difference between you and me, old man, is
> I see the glass half full, you see it half
> empty.

> BLIND MAN
> Night is when you want to sleep, but the
> dry heat keeps you tossin' and turnin'.
> It's when you wish the sun was bakin' high
> in the sky so you could see what it is
> you're afraid of.

> BOBBY
> You afraid of the dark?

> BLIND MAN
> Afraid of it? Boy, I live in the dark. All
> cause of a woman who made me this way.
> People are afraid of what they can't see.
> I can't see nuthin', so it's all the same
> to me. Kiss from a beautiful woman, kissy
> (MORE)

(CONTINUED)

51   CONTINUED: (2)   51

                    BLIND MAN (cont'd)
          kissy kiss, a lick from a dog, slurp,
          slurp, the kiss of death (he makes a
          strange sound). It's all the same to me.

                    BOBBY
          So, we're all just floating along like
          twigs in a stream, so enjoy the ride. Is
          that it?

                    BLIND MAN
          More or less.

                    BOBBY
          Not this twig, friend. I got plans.

                    BLIND MAN
          Nothing makes the Great Spirit laugh harder
          than a man's plans. We all got plans. I
          planned on seeing all my life. I know you
          didn't plan on straying into town.

                    BOBBY
          No and I don't plan on sticking around
          either.

                    BLIND MAN
          Well, don't say I didn't warn you when
          things go your way.

                    BOBBY
          You got a lotta philosophy in you, old
          timer but you don't fool me for one second
          with all this blind man crap. One minute
          you lost your eyes in Vietnam, next it's
          the joint. Now it's a woman? I'm hep to
          you.

The Blind Man slowly lifts his glasses, showing his EYES at
last. Where his eyes should be are scars and dead flesh. An ugly
sight that even takes Bobby back a step.

                    BLIND MAN
          Used to be a young smartass like you. Then
          I got smart with the wrong man's daughter.
          Got some acid poured on my peepers for my
          trouble. You know human beings ain't always
          just human -- they got animals living
          inside 'em too...People give spare change
          to war heroes not fools. All fools get is
          pity. May not have eyes, but I see. And
          you, boy?

The Blind Man puts his glasses back on.

                                              (CONTINUED)

51   CONTINUED: (3)   51

                              BLIND MAN
                    You got my pity.

                              BOBBY (doesn't believe him)
                    Hope she was worth it.

                              BLIND MAN
                    Oh, she was worth it. She was worth every
                    black minute since.

          Bobby looks at his watch, gets ready to go, drops a coin into
          the Blind Man's cup.

                              BOBBY
                    Time's up. Any last words of wisdom?

                              BLIND MAN
                    Things ain't always the way they seem. You
                    got to ask yourself: is it worth it? Day
                    comes Earthmaker is going to look in your
                    fucking heart! Then you better know what it
                    is you're doing. *Are you a human being* --
                    or just one of them hungry ghosts out there
                    floatin' around?

          Bobby walks away, smiling.

                              BOBBY
                    You *are* crazy, you know. Be seeing you, old
                    man.

                              BLIND MAN
                    You know I won't be seeing you.

          The Blind Man lifts his sunglasses and peers into the cup *as if*
          he sees. We don't really know. He reaches into the cup and pulls
          out the coin Bobby tossed in.

                              BLIND MAN
                    Cheap bastard. Gives me back my own
                    money... Well, Jesse, time's up, let's go
                    for a walk.

          The Blind Man now stands up and pulls the seeing-eye dog's
          harness. The DOG struggles to its feet and they walk off down
          the street together.

52   INT. MCKENNA HOUSE - NIGHT   52

          GRACE stands by the back door staring at the bolt lock. JAKE
          yells to her from another room.

52   CONTINUED: 52

                              JAKE(O.C.)
                    What the hell you doin', Grace? Are you
                    coming to bed, or aren't you?

          For a moment Grace's hand wavers above the lock. Suddenly, like
          a snake striking, her hand shoots out and unlocks the bolt.
          Just as quickly she turns from the door and heads to the
          bedroom.

53   EXT. YARD - MCKENNA HOUSE - NIGHT   53

          A LIGHT is on in the bedroom window. After a moment it dims and
          the house is dark, silhouetted against the horizon by moonlight.
          BOBBY steps into frame, carrying an iron pipe.

54   INT. MCKENNA HOUSE/BEDROOM - SIMULTANEOUS   54

          We start close on GRACE -- a KEY slapping against her buttocks
          as bedsprings groan. We reveal Grace copulating on all fours
          with JAKE from behind.

                              JAKE
                    Ya little bitch, you like it don't you! You
                    like it this way -- rough and hard. Gotta
                    go fuck around on me, like your Mama, but
                    you always gotta come home to Daddy, don't
                    you, cause you know Daddy's the best.

                              GRACE
                    Yes, yes, hit me...beat me, please.

                              JAKE
                    You been a bad girl, Grace. You took my
                    heart from your Mama, didn't ya? You
                    betrayed her! Like you did me. There ain't
                    no forgivin' ya, girl!

                              GRACE
                    Oh no! Oh please forgive me, Papa!

                              JAKE
                    You broke her heart! Your broke your Mama's
                    heart. You stole me! That's right. Fuck it
                    away. But it ain't ever goin' away, cause
                    your Mama -- she's like a hungry ghost
                    baby, she won't go away, she won't leave ya
                    alone.

                              GRACE
                    No! No! Please!

          He hits her. Harder.

                                                          (CONTINUED)

54   CONTINUED: 54

In a strange flashback of his mind, he now sees Grace's MAMA
beneath him, receiving his punishment.

He stops, abruptly. He can't go on. Fear coming into his eyes.
He starts to whimper, begging for his punishment and/or
forgiveness.

                    JAKE
          Oh baby, I'm so sorry... I'm so sorry...
              (he starts to cry)
          I didn't mean to hurt you so bad. It
          just...got away...

He drops down, burying his face between Grace's legs.

                    JAKE
          Forgive me, baby, forgive me!

He hides there from the world that he has created, crying to
himself.

Grace has an unreadable expression, but that's certainly not a
new occurrence in their strange relationship.

55   INT. MCKENNA HOUSE/BACKDOOR - NIGHT   55

The knob of the backdoor twists and the door opens. BOBBY slips
quickly through the space and into the house quietly closing the
door behind him. It is nearly pitch dark, and he has no
bearings. He steps gingerly through the hall, but in the
darkness he bumps into a table nearly knocking over a lamp only
to catch it just before it crashes into the floor.

56   INT. MCKENNA HOUSE/BEDROOM - SIMULTANEOUS   56

JAKE hears the noise. He raises his head and cocks an ear to
the air. She knows who it is, and is concerned; he's too early.

                    GRACE
          What's the matter?

                    JAKE
          You didn't hear something?

                    GRACE
          Yeah, I heard a key slapping against my
          ass.

                    JAKE
          There's someone in the house.

                                              (CONTINUED)

56   CONTINUED: 56

                              GRACE (nervous)
                Maybe...maybe the wind blew something over
                (encouraging him to continue). Come on
                baby, keep going.

Jake climbs out of bed, throwing on some pants, reaching into a
drawer in the chest of clothes, pulling out a small dark
metallic OBJECT.

                              GRACE (realizing)
                What's that? Jake -- where'd you get that?

                              JAKE
                Relax baby. Stay here.

He goes to the door. She follows, tries to block the door.

                              GRACE
                Jake, don't go out there. Call the sheriff.

                              JAKE
                Shhhh! Just like your Mama, always scared
                of things...

He maneuvers her aside and slips out the door into the corridor.

57   INT. LIVING ROOM/MCKENNA HOUSE - SIMULTANEOUS   57

Crowbar in one hand, BOBBY makes his way slowly through the
living room, banging against the edge of a table. He hops
silently in pain, then waits at the door to the next room and
listens. Hearing nothing he slowly pokes his head into the
darkness. A moment later Bobby backs from the door and we see
the barrel of his own black .9mm BARETTA pressed against his
forehead. JAKE appears now, backing him into the living room.
He switches on a LAMP.

                              JAKE
                Well, well. As I live and breath. I
                didn't expect to be seeing the likes of you
                again. Thought you'd be long on your way
                by now.

Jake continues to press the gun to Bobby's head.

                              BOBBY
                That's my gun...(then) That fucking
                Darrell!

                              JAKE
                I like Darrell. He may be an idiot, but
                he's my half brother. We own Harlin's
                              (MORE)

                                                              (CONTINUED)

57   CONTINUED: 57

                          JAKE (cont'd)
            together, yeah, that little redneck manages
            to get paid no matter how things work out.

                          BOBBY (realizing)
            You been workin' me the whole time.

                          JAKE
            I guess this is what they call "ironee"?
            Hunh?

                          BOBBY
            It's not what you think, Jake.

                          JAKE
            No, but it don't matter anyway when you're
            lying there with your brains all over my
            carpet and I'm telling Sheriff Potter about
            this drifter, didn't have enough money to
            fix his car. And Darrell happened to find
            his gun, and thought maybe this drifter
            heard old Jake got some money stashed away,
            and figgered he might try to break in and
            steal it!

                          BOBBY
            Wait a minute. Just listen to me...

                          JAKE
            ...And he thought he'd clock old Jake
            McKenna and turn his brains into wall
            paper...and then maybe borrow $200 or
            $20,000, or $200,000...

                          BOBBY (very serious)
            That's not the reason I'm here Jake.

                          JAKE
            There's another reason? It better be good.

58   INT. HALLWAY - SIMULTANEOUS   58

      GRACE makes her way down the hall in a nightgown, and now hides
      in shadow, listening.

                          BOBBY (V.O.)
            I came for Grace.

                          JAKE (V.O.)
            You came to take my wife from me?

59   INT. LIVING ROOM - SIMULTANEOUS   59

                          BOBBY (sincere)
            No. I came to kill her.

60   INT. HALLWAY   60

GRACE'S eyes get real narrow and angry.

>   JAKE (V.O.)
>   Shhh! Liar.

>   BOBBY (V.O.)
>   It's the truth, Jake.

61   INT. LIVING ROOM   61

>   JAKE
>   That's a thick change of heart from this
>   afternoon.

>   BOBBY
>   Maybe I don't like being played, like she
>   played us today. Maybe I don't like that
>   at all, Jake. I'm just pissed enough, maybe
>   I'll rip the neck off my own grandmother.

>   JAKE
>   You have a lot of talk in you, whole lot of
>   talk.

>   BOBBY
>   Damn it, Jake. There is a guy coming to
>   kill me, and if it comes down to me or
>   Grace, then I pick Grace. You were going
>   to give me thirteen-thousand. Give me
>   two-hundred. I'll kill her and dump the
>   body where no one will ever find it. She
>   showed me the perfect place. There won't be
>   enough left for an autopsy. But I need the
>   money. I've got to have the money.

Jake is silent. He takes his time thinking. Finally:

>   JAKE
>   She's in the bedroom.

62   INT. HALLWAY   62

GRACE, distressed, starts backing off towards the bedroom.

63   INT. LIVING ROOM   63

BOBBY stares at the automatic in JAKE's hand.

(CONTINUED)

63   CONTINUED: 63

                         BOBBY
               Wanna give me my gun?

Jake laughs, a "don't even think about it" look.

                         JAKE
               A strangling'll do just fine. Go to work.

Bobby holds up his eight fingers with a "you try" look. Jake
shrugs. Bobby points to the crowbar on the carpet.

                         BOBBY
               How 'bout the pipe?

                         JAKE (sarcastic)
               She's got a slender neck.

Bobby turns and walks towards the bedroom. Jake follows into an
adjoining room.

                         JAKE
               Hold on a second! Come here!

Bobby turns to Jake, who is suddenly extremely upset.

                         JAKE
               How the hell did you know where the
               bedroom's at?

                         BOBBY
               What are you talking about!

                         JAKE (getting closer)
               This morning when I came in on you and
               Grace, you swore you hadn't been near the
               bedroom. Now you make straight for it.

64   INT. HALLWAY   64

GRACE returns to listen. This thing is like a seesaw battle of
wills.

                         BOBBY (V.O.)
               Come on, Jake --

                         JAKE (V.O.)
               Don't Jake me boy! It's a big house. You
               probably didn't even make it out to the
               desert this afternoon...

65   INT. LIVING ROOM   65

JAKE has come right up on BOBBY in a rage.

                                              (CONTINUED)

65   CONTINUED: 65

                          JAKE
          ...Or did you just ply the afternoon away
          between my sheets putting your lips all
          over her, you little horndog...

                          BOBBY (changing tactics)
          What difference does it make if I slept
          with her? We're gonna kill her.

                          JAKE
          You're right! I don't give a damn about
          her. But killing her's one thing. Fucking
          her behind my back, that's another!

Suddenly Jake swings his arm, clipping Bobby across the side of
the head with the pistol and opening another bloody gash.

Bobby crumbles to his knees, crying out.

Jake suddenly grabs Bobby by the hair, forcing his face back and
smearing his lips with his own in a vengeful kiss. The blood
from Bobby's wound runs down to his lips and mixes with Jake's
lips.

                          JAKE
          Now you've tasted *both* of us!

He pulls back the hammer on the gun and levels it at Bobby's
head. Bobby sees it coming, plays his last card on his knees.

                          BOBBY
          O.K.! I admit it! I fucked her! But it's
          her you have to worry about, not *me!* She
          wants you *dead*, Jake. She wants you *dead*
          and she wants your money.

                          JAKE (hesitates)
          What are you babbling about?

                          BOBBY (talking fast)
          Think about it! How do you think I got in
          here? Did you hear any glass break? Did you
          hear a door splinter?

66   INT. HALLWAY - SIMULTANEOUS   66

GRACE listening.

                          BOBBY (V.O.)
          How did the evening end? After you went to
          bed did she linger a bit? Maybe just long
          enough to leave the door unlocked? Is that
          what happened?

67   INT. LIVING ROOM - SIMULTANEOUS   67

Like an old rag, JAKE gradually soaks all this up becoming
heavier with the weight of the knowledge.

                    JAKE
          You'd tell me anything to save your
          pathetic life.

                    BOBBY
          You know what kind of woman Grace is, Jake.
          You know how badly she wants to get the
          fuck out of Superior. What's she to you,
          Jake; a woman who wants you dead? Let me
          kill her. All I want is two-hundred
          dollars to get out of here with.

                    JAKE
          Two-hundred dollars?

                    BOBBY
          Two-hundred dollars...I'll do it! I'll
          kill her!

A beat. Jake stares down at Bobby on the floor.

                    JAKE
          Sweet Christ, I'd be doing the world a
          favor, ridding it of the likes of you. Get
          your miserable ass off the floor. You're
          positively pathetic... Go on, go kill
          Grace.

Bobby slowly stands.

                    JAKE
          I'm not letting you walk for nothing. Two
          hundred dollars. Do it, boy. *Kill her.*

Bobby goes.

68   INT. HALLWAY - SIMULTANEOUS   68

GRACE bolts back to the bedroom, the camera following her as she
flies.

69   INT. BEDROOM HALLWAY - NIGHT (MOMENTS LATER)   69

BOBBY walks it. His POV -- the door. Every step seems freighted.

70   INT. BEDROOM - SIMULTANEOUS   70

GRACE is in a quandary. How many seconds before Bobby walks in
to kill her? Or can he really kill her? She's not sure.

She looks around the room frantically. Picks up a lamp, puts it
down. She looks quickly through her closet, rummages below in
the boxes. Suddenly she finds it.

A dangerous looking Indian HATCHET with a feather hanging off
its bindings. It's a formidable piece of iron, quite capable of
splitting a skull or impaling flesh.

Grace hears the footsteps just outside the door. She runs behind
the door.

A moment later, the bedroom door creaks open and BOBBY quietly
enters, approaching the bed. We sense the doubt in his eyes as
to whether he can kill her.

In a reverse POV, Bobby sees the outline of Grace in the bed as
victim...closer, closer. He now lifts the edge of the bedcover
but sees a blanket bunched up to resemble a human figure.

He suddenly hears a foot fall behind him, then he feels her
presence. He spins.

She's <u>directly</u> <u>behind him</u>, hatchet raised. His life is in her
hands.

His eyes, locked in an eternal moment.

Her eyes, the hatchet.

                                            SNAP CUT TO:

71   INT. HALLWAY - SIMULTANEOUS   71

As JAKE, anxiously torn, waits, there is a LOUD CRASH, followed
by SOUNDS of struggle, of murder, of death. Then...

                    GRACE
          Jake!

It is a desperate cry for help. Jake can't help himself. He
breaks into a roaring run down the hall to save his beloved.

                    JAKE
          Grace!!

72   INT. BEDROOM - SIMULTANEOUS   72

JAKE bulls into the bedroom. It's a mess, furniture overturned,
sheets and blankets all over the floor. The lights broken.
Waiting for him, face down on the floor, is BOBBY'S BODY in a
pool of liquid. A broken bottle lies nearby. Bobby's body heaves
in its final death throes, and then shudders quiet... Over
there, by the bed, is GRACE, who still clutches the HATCHET.
The look on her face is pure shock.

> JAKE
> Well...looks like you got him, Grace.
> That's good...that's real good. He must of
> slipped past me, but you got him. Looks
> like that drifter from this morning. Got
> to be careful who you make friends with,
> sweetheart.

Jake eyes the weapon in Grace's hand.

> JAKE
> Why don't you put that down? It's all over
> now. Put it down.

Grace eyes the gun in Jake's hand.

> JAKE
> Go on, girl. Put it down.

What choice does Grace have? She lets the hatchet clank to the
floor.

> JAKE
> Aww, that's my Grace: Not about to let
> someone get the best of her. That's what I
> love about you. As dangerous as you are
> unpredictable.

Behind Jake, the lifeless BOBBY rises up from the floor, very
much alive, and clobbers Jake with a golf club. Jake is
staggered, but he's one tough old customer as he manages to spin
slowly, gun still in hand, as if to fire.

Before he can, Grace grabs up the hatchet from the floor and
drives it straight into his back.

He gurgles, stunned from both sides, but it's like trying to
kill Rasputin. He still has the gun as Bobby jumps him from the
rear, trying to get his neck in a chokehold. The gun FIRES once,
discharging into the wall. The hatchet is ripped from his back.

(CONTINUED)

CONTINUED:

Grace watches as the two men bang into the walls in a rugged
rodeo-type fight, Jake seeking to dislodge Bobby off his back.
An expression of fear and excitement in her eyes.

Finally the two men go crashing to the ground, rolling around,
Bobby maintaining his stranglehold, but calling to her, his
hands full.

                    BOBBY
          Grace, goddamit, do something!

Jake's eyes roll up at her like a beaching whale, pleading for
help.

                    JAKE
          Grace...?

She commits. Jumping into the fray, it's not clear whose side
she's really on as the three of them roll across the floor,
strangling, biting, hitting, spitting, scratching, gasping. It's
a Guignol, but the pressure from Bobby's forearm is taking its
toll on Jake. Trying to bite Jake, Grace bites Bobby instead,
but then she scratches Jake's face. Jake is grabbing her hard as
Bobby chokes him, trying to use her to leverage himself away.
But she manages to rip herself from his grip and scrambles on
her knees across the floor.

She grabs the hatchet. And stands, moving back towards the two
men locked on the floor. Bobby looks up at her, hatchet in hand,
no longer sure which way she'll go.

Jake, however, gasping for air, eyes bulging, spittle dripping
from his mouth, looks at Grace with some inner certainty that
she will help him. He gasps the words.

                    JAKE
          Help me, Grace, help...

                    GRACE
          Like you helped her, Jake?

Grace stands there, deciding, the power of the hatchet in her
hands. She raises it suddenly over the two men.

It flashes downwards. Deep into the gut of her husband Jake,
almost transfixing him to the floor.

In the silence that follows, Jake's eyes roll up to meet hers.
But all she has for him is a cold, distant stare.

Jake's head drops as the life rushes out of him. Bobby falls
back from the body puffing and dripping with sweat.

                                              (CONTINUED)

                              BOBBY
                 What the hell'd you wait for?

She doesn't answer, turbulence in her face. He rolls Jake's body
off, upset. She may have made it a murder, but he was part of
it, and he feels the shift in himself. They're both in new
territory, feeling an apartness between them.

Suddenly *JAKE gasps*, still alive! It is too much for Bobby. He
grabs the hatchet and plunges it down on Jake, silencing him one
last time.

Grace is pushing the bed away from the wall, slipping down on
her knees and prying open several floorboards.

                              GRACE
                 The money's right here! Get the key!

                              BOBBY
                 No! You get it.

He doesn't want to get close to Jake. Grace coldly runs over to
his corpse, ripping the chain, key and all, from the neck. The
action pulls Jake's head up, then she lets it thump back on the
floor. She runs back to the floorboards.

The top of a thick steel floor safe is revealed.

Bobby watches -- his whole life, it seems, hanging on the
outcome.

With the key, she opens the safe. Inside are rolled-up bundles
of cash -- in hundred dollar denominations. She looks up at him,
offering it as she reaches in for more. Bobby also gets down on
his hands and knees and grabs more and more, sucked into the
fever of freedom, far more money than he lost at the grocery
store, overcome now with emotions of fear and freedom.

They see each other.

                              GRACE
                 Didn't I tell you?

                              BOBBY (plunging into the cash)
                 There must be 150, 200 thousand here!
                 Goddamnit Grace, you were right!

                              GRACE
                 We done it, Bobby. Oh my God!

They laugh excitedly and start kissing, rolling in the stacks of
cash, some of which sticks to Bobby's sweating back. The day
didn't turn out so bad after all for Bobby.

                                                       (CONTINUED)

72   CONTINUED: (3)   72

                              GRACE
                    Fuck me baby!

                              BOBBY (looking at Jake)
                    What about him?

                              GRACE
                    Let him watch. I want him to know what he's
                    missing.

          As they consummate their violent relationship for the first
          time, Jake's lifeless eyes watch them.

73   EXT. MCKENNA HOUSE - LATER NIGHT   73

          The LIGHT in the bedroom window is low candlelight, but we sense
          something watching them. GRACE's silhouette moves across a
          window.

          BOBBY now comes out of the house, cautious, walking down the
          driveway.

          He stops, thinks, and walks back to open the hood of GRACE'S JEEP.

          He reaches into the ENGINE and disconnects something, then
          closes the hood and walks on.

74   EXT. HARLIN'S GARAGE - NIGHT   74

          BOBBY walks up to the SHACK near the garage and bangs on the
          door. A light goes on in the window. DARRELL shouts out.

                              DARRELL (O.C.)
                    What you want?

                              BOBBY
                    Open up!

                              DARRELL (O.C.)
                    We're closed. Come back when the sun comes
                    up.

          Bobby, in a hurry to get back should Grace pull any tricks,
          bangs and kicks against the door. Darrell yanks the door wide.

                              DARRELL
                    What the hell . . . oh, it's you. Might've
                    figgered. Listen I got a waitress coming
                    over. What do you want?

                              BOBBY
                    I want my car.

                                                         (CONTINUED)

> DARRELL
> You got the money?

Bobby pulls the money from his hip pocket and hands it to
Darrell. The mechanic fingers it suspiciously.

> DARRELL
> Two-hundred dollars in hundred-dollar
> bills. And this morning you was broke.

> BOBBY
> That's none of your business. Get the keys.

> DARRELL
> I don't want no dirty money. I run an
> honest business.

> BOBBY
> Yeah, like Al Capone on tax day. Get the keys?

> DARRELL (pause)
> Well, there's a $50 overnight storage
> charge we got to talk about.

Bobby is ready at first to explode, but then just laughs out
loud. You got to give it to a guy like Darrell. He holds up a
$100 bill.

> BOBBY
> All I got's a hundred, Darrell. You got change?

> DARRELL
> No.

> BOBBY
> Figgers. There's a scratch on the hood and how
> much you make selling my gun? Deduct it.

Bobby pulls the hundred back from Darrell's grasp.

> DARRELL (going to get the keys)
> Don't know nothing about no gun.

> BOBBY
> Course you don't. Tell me something
> Darrell. Forty thousand people die every
> day! How come none of them are you?

> DARRELL (throws him the keys)
> I think you know where to find her.

> BOBBY
> And the trunk key.

CONTINUED: (2)

>   DARRELL (pulls out the trunk key)
> Topped off the tank for you. No charge.
> Just my way of doing business.

>   BOBBY (jovial, confident now)
> Listen up good, Darrell. I'm getting outta
> this shithole. You're staying! And one
> little peep outta you -- remember that gun
> makes you part of the food chain. Your
> prints are all over it. I'd be awful
> careful whose rectum I was pointing my
> finger in, Darrell.

Bobby hops in the car, a free man. As Darrell glares at him,
bewildered and frightened at the same time.

75   EXT. MCKENNA HOUSE - NIGHT   75

BOBBY turns the MUSTANG up the drive. The HEADLIGHTS cut the
darkness and land on an empty patch where Grace's jeep had been
parked. Bobby jumps from the Mustang and runs around
frantically. His look is devastated. He falls to his knees,
about to sob when:

GRACE opens the front door and pokes her head out, putting out
several suitcases.

>   GRACE
> Bobby? What the hell's the matter with
> you?

>   BOBBY
> I . . . nothing. I just stubbed my toe on
> a rock. Hurt like hell.

>   GRACE
> I got the money all packed. I put the jeep
> and his caddy in the garage. People'll
> think maybe me and Jake went away. Buy us
> some time...I know a back road we can take.

>   BOBBY
> Good thinking. (looking at her four bags)
> What's all this?

>   GRACE
> I'm not coming back.

>   BOBBY (accepting)
> Awright, let's go. I want to be fifty miles
> from here before the sun comes up.

75   CONTINUED: 75

                              GRACE
                    Funny thing; the jeep wouldn't start. I had
                    to push it.

                              BOBBY (dryly)
                    Funny thing... I'll get the bags.

76   EXT. MCKENNA HOUSE - LATER NIGHT   76

Bobby's MUSTANG is backed towards the front of the house. We
see a silhouette of BOBBY and GRACE carrying something wrapped
in a BLANKET and dumping it in the trunk.

77   EXT. DESERT HIGHWAY - NIGHT   77

A lone pair of HEADLIGHTS illuminate the night as the Mustang
cruises through the dark. As the lights brighten the screen we:

                                                  FADE TO:

78   INT./EXT. MUSTANG - NIGHT   78

GRACE sits next to BOBBY peering out the windshield, clutching
the money in a backpack. She's humming an Indian song.

                              BOBBY
                    I can't see it.

                              GRACE
                    It should be just up ahead. Hold on . . .
                    there! There it is!

A SIGN illuminated by the HEADLIGHTS.. It reads: YOU ARE
LEAVING SUPERIOR. THANKS FOR VISITING.

GRACE lets out a scream of joy, leans over and hugs him.

                              GRACE
                    Oh, God! I can't believe it. I'm out.
                    I'm finally out!

The MUSTANG begins to swerve along the road.

                              BOBBY
                    Hey! Take it easy. Want to get us killed?

                              GRACE
                    You don't know what it feels like to be
                    free of that place.

                              BOBBY
                    I don't know about that?

                                                    (CONTINUED)

                    GRACE
          You spent a day in Superior. I wasted my
          entire life there. I feel like someone just
          took a million pounds off my shoulders.

                    BOBBY
          We've still got some dead weight to get rid of.

                    GRACE
          Can't we just dump him fast someplace?

                    BOBBY
          I want a place where only the vultures will
          find him...(then) It'll be over soon,
          Grace.

                    GRACE
          Then will you take me on your friends' boat
          with you?

                    BOBBY
          I'm not sailing his boat.

                    GRACE
          But I thought --

                    BOBBY
          We're going to buy a boat of our own baby,
          and sail it wherever we want to go.

                    GRACE
          Anywhere?

                    BOBBY
          What the hell? Why not? Where should we go?

                    GRACE
          Hawaii. I've read all about it. I've
          dreamed of going there and just lying on
          the beach while the water licked up against
          my feet. Oh, God. I'd kill to go there.

                    BOBBY
          You already have.

She gives him a funny look.

                    BOBBY
          You know I thought you'd left me back
          there.

                    GRACE
          What are you talking about?

                                              (CONTINUED)

                              BOBBY (emotional)
When I got back from the garage, and your
jeep wasn't there, I thought you'd gone and
left me and taken the money.
          (off her look)
...Cause I never had any luck with women,
Grace. You don't know what I been through.
The shit I've taken. I thought you were
like the rest of 'em... but when you came
out of the house... well you're here Grace
and we might be starting in the shit but
we're starting where I never been --
together with *someone* -- together with *you*
Grace.

She responds with a luminous smile.

                              GRACE
I love you Bobby.

He looks back at her with trust and love in his eyes.

                              BOBBY
We're gonna pull this off, Grace.

Just then a HEADLIGHT rakes them from the rear as we hear,
again, the ominous crackle of a POLICE RADIO and the short
brutal "Whoop" of the siren, as Sheriff Potter's VEHICLE rolls
up quickly behind them. Grace's face is caught like a surprised
deer in the headlamps.

                              GRACE
Oh, my God!
          (then)
Don't stop!

Bobby is in a bind. The siren whoops again. The lights flash to
highbeam.

                              BOBBY
He must've seen us swerving on the road,
that's all, just gonna give us a ticket for
swerving...

But even Bobby has trouble believing that as the POLICE VEHICLE
pulls out sharply alongside his and SHERIFF POTTER motions to
him aggressively to pull over on the shoulder.

                         SHERIFF (into loudspeaker)
Pull over, goddamnit, pull over!

                              GRACE
Keep going!

                                            (CONTINUED)

She seems to be panicking. Bobby pulls over.

>   BOBBY
>   Fuck this!...Just shut up, Grace. We done
>   nothing! Be cool. Let me do the talking. He
>   doesn't know anything.

His vehicle pulled up on the shoulder in front of them, the
Sheriff gets out, shining his power flashlight into their faces.

>   BOBBY (starts)
>   'Evening Sheriff, sorry bout that but this
>   jackrabbit...

Bobby has no time to react as the Sheriff is suddenly there at
his window, jerking his door open, angry. A GUN in his hand,
pointed at them, his eyes on Grace.

>   SHERIFF
>   You had to *fuck him*, didn't you!

>   GRACE (nervous cool)
>   I would never do that to you, baby... He
>   killed Jake -- said he'd kill me if I
>   didn't come with him. All he wants is the
>   money.

Bobby looks at her. He cannot believe what he just heard.

>   BOBBY
>   What!

>   SHERIFF (flipping, yelling)
>   *Don't lie to me!*

Grace knows the jam is up.

>   GRACE
>   OK...but he never made me cum! Really
>   Virgil, I was only doing what I had to do
>   so we could be free. Just like we talked
>   about. It meant *nothing.*

A pause. Virgil wants to kill her, but he also wants her back
badly.

>   BOBBY
>   You fucking him too Grace? Is everybody
>   fucking everybody in this town?

She ignores him. Her attention on the backpack with the money
between her legs -- the gun is there, inside an outer flap of
the bag.

                                                   (CONTINUED)

> SHERIFF
> You fuck this guy -- get him to do your
> dirty work and you think you can take the
> money and dump me?

> GRACE
> No baby, you got it wrong.

> SHERIFF
> This road don't go to Globe, Grace -- where
> were you going to meet me?

His flashlight on the four suitcases in the backseat. She
doesn't have an answer to that one.

> GRACE
> It's not like that it... Look, Virgil, I
> got the money here.

She gets out of the car on her side, comes around to him, the
pack of money slung on her shoulder, hard to see in the dark.

> SHERIFF (hurt)
> Oh Grace, you can say what you want...but,
> I watched you fuck that pervert for years
> while you're telling me you loved me? What
> happened to going to Milwaukee together?
> You and me -- gonna open up the finest
> sporting goods store that city ever did
> see? Get us a place on the north shore, by
> the lake? Season Brewer tickets! Just you
> and me, Grace. What happened?

> GRACE
> All talk, that's all you did was talk, and
> all I did was sit around getting older
> waiting for you to free me! You never did
> nothin' Virgil, you're weak! (pointing to
> Bobby) *He did!*

The Sheriff, deeply wounded, casts a hot vicious gaze on Bobby.

> SHERIFF
> This is some girl you and me got here
> Bobby, yessir, an excellent cocksuck too,
> wouldn't you say? (back at Grace)... Course
> you had a lotta practice haven't you
> darling, going way back to your crazy mama!

> GRACE (deadly)
> Shut up, Virgil! Take your share of the
> money. It's not so bad.

                              SHERIFF
          I don't want the fuckin' money! I'm not
          gonna give up everything I got for a lousy
          50,000 dollars. It's *you*. You *Grace or*
          nothing. The whole thing... I want you to
          be my wife...(hopeful). What do you say
          Grace?

                              GRACE
          You sound just like Jake... I did see into
          the future, Virgil, but you weren't in it.
          Go back to your family. They love you.

Bobby gets out of the car, misunderstanding the situation.

                    BOBBY (misunderstanding)
          Look, we got more. We got $200,000 at
          least. Split it three ways, we all walk
          away...

The Sheriff snaps and smashes Bobby with his flashlight,
knocking him to the ground, kicking him again and again,
gathering the psychic force to murder him. Grace tries to
approach.

                              SHERIFF
          Shut up, boy! You don't know shit round
          here! (to Grace) Get back. Did she tell you
          that story about the bird flying away?

                    BOBBY (rolling on the ground)
          Ow! Look, I ... ow!

                              GRACE
          Stop! Stop it!

                    SHERIFF (kicking again and again)
          Were you going to help her fly away,
          asshole? What'd you think, you were the
          first boy to drift through this town she
          came on to? She tell you the story about
          old Jake forcing her to marry him? That's a
          good story... How he killed her crazy Mama?

Bobby in bloody agony. Grace stunned that Virgil would reveal
this now publicly.

                              GRACE
          Goddamit Virgil, stop! Don't!

78   CONTINUED: (6)   78

                              SHERIFF
                    ...But I bet the story she *didn't* tell you
                    was the best story of all. How old crazy
                    Jake *was really her Papa*. And she *liked*
                    fucking Papa! And now she's killed the
                    sonufabitch! Just like she's gonna kill
                    you!

Grace plunges into the pack, pulls the gun and shoots Virgil
across the car in the gut.

                              GRACE
                    No...you! You!

The Sheriff flies back onto the road, stunned, not realizing
what's happened.

Bobby watches unbelieving as Grace quietly steps up over the
Sheriff.

She puts the next round in his nuts, a modern fury enacting
ancient wrath.

                              BOBBY
                    Grace. No!

The Sheriff is wide-eyed, dying in shock. Grace then fires right
at his head in a coup de grace that blows his brains out the
back of his head.

Grace and Bobby both stare, then Grace jumps into action,
dragging the body. She snaps at Bobby.

                              GRACE
                    Help me get him off the road. Into the car!
                    We'll ditch his car... Get the fuck up!

Bobby stares at her.

79   EXT./INT. MUSTANG - NIGHT   79

They're driving. GRACE and BOBBY, wordless, each thinking in
separate worlds. Grace wipes her hands. The bag with the money
between her legs. The Baretta is back in the bag.

                              BOBBY (finally)
                    Jesus, did you have to kill him?

                              GRACE
                    Get real Bobby. He was gonna kill you *and*
                    me.

                                                        (CONTINUED)

                    BOBBY
          He was in love with you Grace. He would've
          done what you wanted, you could've made a
          deal and ...

                    GRACE
          The only deal he had in mind was killing
          you for Jake's murder and blackmailing me
          into sucking his dick for the rest of my
          life... no thanks.

                    BOBBY
          He was a *cop*, Grace, they never stop
          looking for you when you kill a cop...

                    GRACE
          He was a scumbag!... He wanted *me*, Bobby.
          These guys don't let go! Even when they're
          dead... (softer) You don't know what it was
          like, Bobby. Those two, they were the same.

A silence. The oncoming road.

                    GRACE
          So, aren't you going to ask me?

                    BOBBY
          Ask you what? You mean what kind of
          horrifying sick shit is coming next?

                    GRACE
          Don't you want to know...? I bet it's
          burning a hole in your brain just now?

                    BOBBY
          Let it go, baby. It's the past. I got a
          past...

                    GRACE
          Don't you really want to know? Was Jake my
          Daddy? Was I fucking my own Daddy? Don't
          you want to know that?

                    BOBBY (shouting)
          What do you want me to say!

She's yelling, emotionally out of control.

                    GRACE
          Yes! I was! I was fucking Daddy! And I
          married him!... I married him...okay?

She looks at Bobby, forces him to look at her. Finally:

                                              (CONTINUED)

                                    BOBBY
                    Why?

                                    GRACE
                    I don't know why!

She drops back in her seat. Tears come.

                                    GRACE
                    All I wanted was to be a kid... He took
                    that from me... They all did... (very
                    quietly, dangerously) They treated me like
                    meat. A piece of meat. *Fuck me. Blow me.*
                    Bend over. Stick their fingers up my ass...
                    Fuck them! Fuck the whole town! They
                    deserved to die!

A pause.

                                    BOBBY
                    And us Grace? What do we deserve?

                                    GRACE (crying quietly to herself)
                    "Nin chonk, nin chonk," my Mama used to say
                    in Apache. "Your worst is doing this to
                    you," she said, "your worst has killed
                    you." And "Be go tsee" -- "you will find
                    out the result of what you have done..."
                    Just when you think it's over, when you've
                    gotten away, it begins. Cause you never get
                    away.

Bobby stares straight ahead at the oncoming road. Can he still
love her? She seems to be reading his thoughts, like she said
she could.

                                    GRACE
                    It's easy to judge someone else when you
                    don't know nothing about it... I'm Apache,
                    Bobby. You don't eat what I eat. You don't
                    see what I see. Don't judge me.

A silence. Two former lovers in the dark of a car moving through
the strangeness of an Arizona desert at night.

                                    BOBBY
                    I don't want to think anymore.

                                    GRACE (quietly)
                    Then drive...

                                                          (CONTINUED)

CONTINUED: (3)

The lights of the car fade until there is nothing but darkness.

                                          THE SUN COMES UP:

EXT. CANYON - END SPOT - DAWN

In the vast reaches of a deserted canyon, where VULTURES circle
in a hot white sky, we find the MUSTANG parked at the edge of a
drop. We hear the SOUND of a body being dragged.

                    D.J. (V.O.)
          ...Nobody's sure where it was heading so
          fast but the way it hit the semi, it won't
          be getting home now! Hey area weather is
          gonna be hot! Hot! Hot! Then cold! Cold!
          Cold! Just like yesterday. Just like every
          day. Some surprise, huh? So if you're
          planning on anything, *don't*. You don't like
          the weather, just wait one minute. Got any
          brains, get up to Alaska and get yourself
          some trailer park where you don't see no
          desert for miles and miles...

                    BOBBY (over)
          Right there... Drop it there. I got it.

BOBBY is giving GRACE instructions as they drop SHERIFF VIRGIL
POTTER'S corpse over a drop onto some rocks 30 yards below.

                    GRACE
          See ya, Virgil. God bless.

Bobby pushes him over, his hand hurting. The body crashes below.
It's hard work. They head back for the Mustang, to retrieve
JAKE'S body in the popped trunk. But Grace notices Bobby
glancing at the Baretta now tucked in her waist.

The silence is tense between them, the rocks and gravel
crunching under their shoes as they walk.

                    GRACE (indicates the gun)
          Is this what's bothering you Bobby?

                    BOBBY
          No Grace, my hand's bothering me.

                    GRACE
          You think now that Jake's dead, there's all
          that money there and I don't need you
          anymore, and I might just sneak up behind
          you sometime and...pop!

                                                    (CONTINUED)

She pulls an imaginary trigger on Bobby, mimicking the recoil of
a gun. Bobby is nervous.

> GRACE
> Don't you think I would've done it if I wanted
> to? What can I do to make you relax, baby?

> BOBBY
> You could give me my gun back.

Grace smiles.

> GRACE
> Why don't we just finish what we started.

She stares down at Jake. She can't help feeling some old
feelings. As Bobby walks back to the front of the car, turns off
the annoying radio. He watches as she softly prays over Jake,
whose face is concealed by the blanket in which he is rolled.

> GRACE (after a moment with Jake)
> What do you think happens to someone's
> spirit when you die?

> BOBBY
> I think nothing happens. You're dead meat.
> That's it.

> GRACE
> You don't believe in anything do you,
> Bobby?

> BOBBY
> I believe in this moment, that's all. There
> is nothing else.
>   (lifting Jake by the shoulder)
> Come on. He must weigh 300 pounds.

Grace leans into the trunk to take his boots when he makes his
move, quickly, closing on her when she's off guard. He slams her
hard in the face, coldly sending her sprawling to the ground,
dazed.

He steps over her and grabs the gun in her waist, checks it.

She puts her hand to her mouth, feels the blood on her finger
tips. She looks at him and laughs a wild crazed laugh that cuts
into Bobby like a knife.

> GRACE
> You hit me, Bobby? You hit a woman, you
> motherfucker! Didn't your Momma ever teach
> you anything...?

(CONTINUED)

Her eyes go to the gun in his hand and she stops laughing. Her
calm is extraordinary, as if expecting to die.

                    GRACE
         Well?

For a moment, Bobby does nothing, then he slips the gun through
his belt.

                    BOBBY
         Well, nothing. We dump Jake, we split the
         money, then you're on your own.

                    GRACE
         Don't leave me. I want to stay with you,
         Bobby.

                    BOBBY
         Why? So when the cops catch up with us you
         can sell me out again?

                    GRACE
         I was just baiting him! Bobby, I had to
         tell him that to get his guard down. Just
         like you told Jake you was going to kill
         me!

                    BOBBY
         You lied to me all along! Lies, all lies.
         Your mother, your father, what story are
         you on now? How come the town didn't know
         you was his daughter?

                    GRACE (in pain)
         Cause my Mom slept around. A lotta men!
         Anybody could've been my father. But *we
         knew*.

                    BOBBY (not listening)
         Well you got what you wanted all along by
         fucking me. I wish you had told me the
         goddamn truth in the first place!

                    GRACE (screws out)
         I didn't *want* you to know! Don't you...
         unnerstand?

Bobby's got a headache now. It's too much to understand, too
much talk. Too much history has taught him to doubt.

                    BOBBY
         When you're finished with me, I'm next! I
         been there, baby. I been there with other
                    (MORE)

                                              (CONTINUED)

80   CONTINUED: (3)   80

                    BOBBY (cont'd)
          cunts...sorry, not anymore. I'll take you
          as far as California. If we can make that.
          After that you're on your own. Try Mexico.
          With all this bread, you can live like a
          queen.

                    GRACE
          I don't want to go to Mexico, Bobby!
          Please, I really want to be with you. Don't
          blow this. Don't you think I care about
          you?

                    BOBBY
          I think you're a lying, back-stabbing
          psycho bitch, and one day you'll kill me.
          But it's nice to know you cared...

The expression on Grace's face changes as rapidly as the desert
weather, a coldness passing over and through her.

                    GRACE
          You don't know your own mind. It blocks
          your heart.

Keeping a wary eye on Grace, Bobby starts hauling Jake out of
the trunk.

                    BOBBY
          Give me a hand.

He wrestles Jake up to a sitting position. He grabs a can of
beer from a warm six-pack in the trunk and shoves it into a
pocket of Jake's coat.

                    BOBBY
          Poor old Jake, a few drinks, a fight with
          the sheriff over his wife. And both of 'em
          ended up dead.

Grace takes his boots.

                    BOBBY
          Time to go for a walk, Jake.

                    GRACE
          My mother died in this canyon.

                    BOBBY
          Save the Mom routine, will ya Grace. It
          doesn't work with me. One, two, three...

They lift the corpse, and with great effort, haul it towards the
edge of the drop. As they pause on the way, Bobby, wary of

                                                  (CONTINUED)

CONTINUED: (4)

Grace's strange coldness, tries to soften the blow of
separation.

> BOBBY
> Look, it's not so bad we split up. It might
> be months before they find these guys. If
> at all. I mean with the mountain lions
> around here. Remember, if they can't find
> no bodies, there's no crime... (She doesn't
> respond.) We'll be in Phoenix by noon. Lose
> this car, get another one. Texas, Mexico
> are big countries, all that money Grace,
> you'll meet someone else, you know, there's
> a lot of hope with a $100,000...

They lift Jake again, and move to the edge.

> GRACE
> Hope is a four letter word.

> BOBBY
> But we all need that too. Hold him.

He props Jake at the edge, standing, and transfers the weight
onto Grace. Jake's head is on her shoulder.

> BOBBY
> You make a pretty couple.

It seems he might push them both over but instead takes the gun,
wipes it of his prints, and slips it through Jake's belt.

> BOBBY
> Won this in a poker game in Reno. God knows
> who it's registered to. You shoulda been
> more careful, Jake. See you later.

As he takes Jake's weight off Grace and pushes it over the drop.

Grace watches him go, her eyes shifting to Bobby, his back
momentarily to her, also watching. She moves towards him.

Bobby turns, slips on the edge.

> BOBBY
> Now all we got to do is try *and*--

He feels a blur of motion, almost like a bird, and he is
falling...falling, his life coming to an end.

Grace is standing somewhere up above, briefly seen. Did she push
him? He doesn't know.

He's stunned as he falls on the rocks next to the bodies of Jake
and Virgil. He screams out in sharp pain. His leg feels broken.
But he is alive.

Grace walks away, cutting it all off, deeply shaken. She must
get away from the past and all these hollow men. She closes the
trunk of the Mustang, gets in the driver's seat, reaches for the
ignition key. Her hand fumbles for it a moment. It isn't there.

                    GRACE
          Shit!

She sits there. Bobby is calling from below.

                    BOBBY
          Grace! Help me, Grace...! We been through
          too much together. We've only had one day,
          but you and me have been through more than
          most people ever will. I know you were
          angry at me, and, you know, you were right!
          I'm sorry I hit you. I was wrong about
          leaving you. You don't belong in Mexico.

She finally gets out and walks back to the edge of the cliff,
looks down.

                    BOBBY
          Thank you. Thank you. I...I knew you
          wouldn't leave me, Grace.

                    GRACE
          Bobby? Are you all right?

                    BOBBY
          I busted my leg!

                    GRACE
          Can you make it back up?

                    BOBBY
          Grace -- in the trunk of my car is a tow
          rope. It should reach down here. Go get it,
          throw it down.

She looks. Of course the trunk is closed. She closed it.

                    GRACE
          Bobby, the trunk...it's locked. Throw the
          keys up to me. I'll get the rope.

Bobby's eyes pass over Jake a few feet away, his eyes staring
upwards in death. They take in the gun still attached to his
waist. He knows the trunk wasn't locked when they took Jake out.

                                                        (CONTINUED)

> BOBBY
> I can't throw that far. You got to climb
> down here and get the keys. You can make
> it. It's the only way Grace.

Grace looks down at the drop. It's a tough descent but she
knows she could make it and get back up as well.

> BOBBY
> Grace!...Please, Grace! You have to help
> me.

Grace takes a look around.

> GRACE
> Okay. I'm coming. Calm down!

She starts down the cliff face. As she descends, he talks
deliriously.

> BOBBY (off)
> I knew you'd help me. I knew you wouldn't
> leave me baby, cause we're tied together
> too close. We belong together always.

Grace makes it to the bottom of the drop, and walks cautiously
towards Bobby.

> GRACE (yelling back, echoing)
> Bobby! Don't flip out on me. I can't do
> this alone. I know you don't trust me, but
> you gotta pull yourself together, I'm not
> gonna leave you...I never wanted it to go
> down like this. It was different with you
> Bobby. You had dreams like me. You
> listened... I would've gone anywhere with
> you, Bobby. We can make this work. I'm
> sorry...I really am. I didn't wanna hurt
> you.

Can he believe her? She sounds so sincere this time.

She's heading for the body of Jake. And the gun. Bobby knows
that and is already crawling there.

> BOBBY (as he crawls)
> They're right here, Grace. The keys. Come
> get me out of here... Know why else I could
> never leave you?

> GRACE
> Why's that?

                              BOBBY
                    'Cause I love you.

Inching closer.

Closer. They meet at the apex of Jake's corpse.

                              GRACE
                    And I love you too.

                              BOBBY
                    And love's a funny thing. Sometimes I
                    don't know if I want to love you...

Grace leans close to Bobby. He dangles the keys out in front of
her, but she doesn't reach for them. Her eyes go to Bobby. She
reaches for him. At that instant Bobby's hands shoot out and
clamp hard around her. A sharp gurgle is all that escapes Grace
as Bobby twists the life from her, as Jake leers up at them.

                              BOBBY
                    ...or kill you.

Grace twists and flails in Bobby's hands, but in spite of his
bleeding stump, he holds her like a bear trap holds a grizzly.

                              BOBBY
                    I love you Grace, but *I just can't trust
                    you!*

She looks at him, trying to protest, shaking her head. Grace's
flailing goes into overdrive. Somewhere in his semi-delirious
state, Bobby's eyes might notice the gun at Jake's waist is no
longer there.

Grace manages one word:

                              GRACE
                    Jake...

                              BOBBY
                    He *can't* help you now, honey!

Bobby is in agony as he kills her, part beast, part lover, he
kills that which he loves.

Suddenly, a SHOT is heard. Bobby buckles with the blast, hit in
the side. He kills her with one last wrenching thrust of his
hands, breaking her neck.

Bobby looks down at Jake's gun, which she clutches in her hand,
and sees the hole in his side and the river of blood that flows

                                                      (CONTINUED)

from it. He manages to stand, looks at Jake; their bodies lying side by side.

Bobby, with great difficulty, claws his way back up the rocks to the car, his fast-flowing wound staining the white rocks with blood.

He makes it to the top and, losing more blood, climbs into the driver's seat. He checks the money in the bag. All there. All his.

As he pulls a huge clot of blood from his side, the vultures circle. Perhaps one, smarter than the others, lands close by. It spooks Bobby but he's okay. He looks in the mirror.

                    BOBBY
          You're still lucky.

He puts the car key in the ignition, the engine comes to life.

                    BOBBY (waves back)
          Adios --

Suddenly, the RADIATOR HOSE Darrell installed blows apart loudly. Bobby knows exactly and immediately what it is as a cloud of steam now rolls from under his hood. He shakes his head, frustrated.

                    BOBBY (sighs)
          Oh shit!...(then) Arizona.

He can't help but laugh at his bad luck. As we rise off the desert floor and take flight with the vultures, eventually leaving them all as specks of earth in the vast empty canyons of Arizona.

                         THE END

STILLS

Robert Richardson, director of photography, and Oliver Stone on Superior's Main Street.

BOBBY COOPER
Sean Penn

GRACE McKENNA
Jennifer Lopez

125

JAKE McKENNA
Nick Nolte

DARRELL
Billy Bob Thornton

SHERIFF VIRGIL POTTER
Powers Boothe

THE BLIND MAN
Jon Voight

The hard luck gambler, Bobby Cooper *(Sean Penn),* arrives in Superior, Arizona.

Oliver Stone discussing a scene with Jon Voight, as Sean Penn prepares himself in the foreground.

Jon Voight, Oliver Stone, and Sean Penn confer on the set of *U-Turn*.

Left: Bobby *(Penn)* listening to the Blind Man.
Right: Grace *(Jennifer Lopez)* and Bobby *(Penn)* first meet.

Grace *(Lopez)* seductively tempts Bobby Cooper at her house.

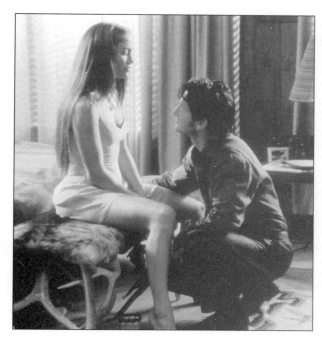

Left: Grace *(Lopez)* tells Bobby's *(Penn)* fortune.

Bobby *(Penn)* walks back to town from Grace's house.

Left: Bobby *(Penn)*, down on his luck and out of money, orders a beer and waits out the heat in a diner.
Right: Toby 'TNT' Tucker *(Joaquin Phoenix)*.

Jenny *(Claire Danes)* and Toby *(Phoenix)* try to vent their frustrations on Bobby *(Penn)*.

Set-up shot for Bobby *(Penn)* pushing Grace *(Lopez)* over the edge of the plateau.

Bobby *(Penn)* grabbing Grace *(Lopez)* at Apache Leap.

Grace *(Lopez)* and Bobby *(Penn)* embrace on Apache Leap, high above Superior.

Grace *(Lopez)* tries to convince Bobby *(Penn)* to help her, after making love near Apache Leap.

Jake *(Nick Nolte)* threatens Bobby with Bobby's own gun when he discovers Bobby breaking into his house.

Bobby *(Penn)* and Grace *(Lopez)* decide how to dispose of the bodies and make their escape from Superior.

Bobby *(Penn)* and Grace *(Lopez)*, wary of each other.

At the canyon edge, the moment of truth comes for Bobby *(Penn)* and Grace *(Lopez)*.

CAST AND CREW CREDITS

PHOENIX PICTURES PRESENTS

An Illusion Entertainment Group Production

In Association With Clyde is Hungry Films

An Oliver Stone Movie

Sean Penn   Jennifer Lopez   Nick Nolte

U-TURN

Starring

Powers Boothe   Claire Danes
Joaquin Phoenix   Billy Bob Thornton
and Jon Voight

Also Starring

Abraham Benrubi   Julie Hagerty
Bo Hopkins   Valery Nikolaev

Casting by
Mary Vernieu

Co-Producer
Richard Rutowski

Costumes Designed by
Beatrix Aruna Pasztor

Music Composed, Orchestrated, and Conducted by
Ennio Morricone

Executive Music Producer
Budd Carr

Edited by
Hank Corwin
Thomas J. Nordberg

Production Designer
Victor Kempster

Director of Photography
Robert Richardson, ASC

Executive Producer
John Ridley

Produced by
Dan Halsted
Clayton Townsend

Screenplay by
John Ridley
Based on the book *Stray Dogs* by John Ridley

Directed by
Oliver Stone

Unit Production Manager . . . . . . Clayton Townsend	First Assistant Editors . . . . Christine Lee
1st Assistant Director . . . . Seth Cirker	Paul Martinez
2nd Assistant Director . . . . Paul Prenderville	Assistant Editor . . . . Yvonne Valdez
Associate Producer . . . . Bill Brown	Supervising Sound Editor . . . . David Kneupper
Controller . . . . Barbara-Ann Stein	ADR Supervisor . . . . Neal J. Anderson
Additional Editors . . . . Brian Berdan	Re-Recording Mixers . . . . Scott Millan
Saar Klein	Brad Sherman
Production Supervisor . . . . Jeff Flach	Key Make-Up Artist . . . . John Blake
Script Supervisor . . . . Corey B. Yugler	Make-Up Artist . . . . Mark R. Sanchez
Stunt Coordinator . . . . Tierre Turner	Jon Voight's Make-up Designed and Created
First Assistant Camera . . . . Gregor Tavenner	by . . . . Ken Diaz
Second Assistant Camera . . . . Jeanne Lipsey	Hair Designer . . . . Cydney Cornell
Video Wrangler . . . . Marty Kassab-Chaney	Hair Stylist . . . . Melissa A. Yonkey
B Camera Operator/2nd Unit DP . . . Jerry G. Calla-	Jon Voight's Hair Stylist . . . . Dino Ganziano
way, S.O.C.	Costume Supervisor . . . . Michelle Kurpaska
Still Photographer . . . . Zade Rosenthal	Sound Mixer . . . . Gary Alper
Set Decorator . . . . Merideth Boswell	Boom Operator . . . . Keith Gardner
Art Director . . . . Dan Webster	Utility Sound . . . . Kevin Cerchiai
Lead Man . . . . Tommy Samona	Chief Lighting Technician . . . . Jonathan Lumley
Coordinator . . . . Sarah Bowen	Assistant Chief Lighting Technician . . Timothy Healy

Key Grip . . . . James Finnerty, Jr.
Best Boy Grip . . . . Tom Kerwick
Property Master . . . . Bill Petrotta
Assistant Property Master . . . . . Michael R. Gannon
Assistant Props . . . . Kevin M. Gannon
Special Effects Coordinator . . . . Mark Hendersheid
Music Editor . . . . Bill Abbott
Assistant Music Editor . . . . Denise Okimoto
Dialogue Editors . . . . Laura Harris
Pat Sellers
Sound Effects Editors . . . . Brian McPherson
Chris Hogan
Fred Stahly
Assistant Sound Editor . . . . Horace Manzanares
Transportation Coordinator . . . . A. Welch Lambeth
Transportation Captains . . . . Jeff Couch
Brian Steagall
Production Coordinator . . . . Gary R. Wordham
Assistant Production Coordinator . . . Karen O'Toole
First Assistant Accountant . . . . Sue Schnulle Murphy
Casting Associates . . . . Anne McCarthy
Alyssa Weisberg
Extras Casting . . . . Sandra Noriega
Assistant to Mr. Stone . . . . . . Annie Mei-Ling Tien
Assistant to Mr. Townsend . . . . Ann Marie DiGioia
Assistant to Mr. Halsted . . . . Mindy Cole
Publicity . . . . Stephen Rivers & Associates
Producers' Representative . . . . Arthur Manson
Assistant Location Manager . . . . David Pomier
Craft Service . . . . Concepcion Roca
Construction Coordinator . . . . Bill Holmquist
Lead Scenic . . . . John A. Kelly
Key Set Production Assistant . . . . Brad Hall
Set Production Assistants . . . James "Morris" Byrnes
Denis Doyle
Gregg Rosenzweig
Larry A. Zience
Office Production Assistants . . . . Ian Calip
Eddie Kish
Stephen Banta
Gary Thomas Williams
Phillip M. Lozevski
Post Production Assistant . . . . Charles Johnston

CAST
(in order of appearance)

Bobby Cooper . . . . Sean Penn
Darrell . . . . Billy Bob Thornton
Biker #1 . . . . Abraham Benrubi
Biker #2 . . . . Richard Rutowski
Blind Man . . . . Jon Voight
Grace McKenna . . . . Jennifer Lopez
Sheriff Potter . . . . Powers Boothe
Jake McKenna . . . . Nick Nolte

Jamilla . . . . Aida Linares
Boy in Grocery Store . . . . Sean Stone
Sergi . . . . Ilia Volokh
Mr. Arkady . . . . Valery Nikolaev
Boyd . . . . Brent Briscoe
Ed . . . . Bo Hopkins
Flo . . . . Julie Hagerty
Short Order Cook . . . . Annie Mei-Ling Tien
Toby N. Tucker . . . . Joaquin Phoenix
Jenny . . . . Claire Danes
Grace's Mother . . . . Sheri Foster
Bus Station Clerk . . . . Laurie Metcalf
Girl in Bus Station . . . . Liv Tyler

STOCK FOOTAGE PROVIDED BY:
BBC Worldwide Americas, Inc.
Imagebank
SFV International

SPECIAL THANK YOU
Kalil Bottling Company; Dr. Pepper/Seven Up, Inc.;
Movado Watch Company; Rimrock Natural
Water Co.; City of Superior, Arizona;
Kevin C. White, Gary S. Greene

In Association with Canal+ Droits Audiovisuels

Time Lapse Photography . . . . . Wayne D. Goldwyn
Negative Cutting . . . . . . Donah Bassett & Associates
Color Timer . . . . Bob Kaiser
Lighting and Equipment by . . . . Paskal Lighting
Sound Design by . . . . Soundelux
Music Recorded at . . . . Forum Music Village–Rome
Re-Recording Services . . . Todd A O Studios West
Color & Prints by . . . . Technicolor®
Titles and Opticals by . . . . Pacific Title

Soundtrack on Epic

MUSIC

"It's A Good Day"
Written by Peggy Lee and Dave Barbour
Performed by Peggy Lee
Courtesy of Capitol Records under license from
EMI-Capitol Music Special Markets

"Help Me Make It Through The Night"
Written by Kris Kristofferson
Performed by Sammi Smith
Courtesy of Sizemore Music by arrangement with
Celebrity Licensing, Inc.

"II B.S."
Written and Performed by Charles Mingus
Courtesy of MCA Records by arrangement with
Universal Music Special Markets

"Hebba Ho"
"Meatgrinder"
Written by tim floyd tim
Performed by Ditch Croaker
Courtesy of Reprise Records by arrangement with
Warner Special Products

"Largo Al Factotum" from "The Barber of Seville"
Written by Gioacchino Rossini
Arranged by Lee Ashley
Vocal by David Romano
Music Courtesy of OGM/OLE GEORG MUSIC,
Hollywood, CA

"Piss Up A Rope"
Written by Michael Melchiondo and Aaron Freeman
Performed by Ween
Courtesy of Elektra Entertainment Group by
arrangement with Warner Special Products

"More And More"
Written by Merle Kilgore
Performed by Webb Pierce
Courtesy of MCA Records by arrangement with
Universal Music Special Markets

"La Mujer Que Amas"
Written by B. Adams, M. Kamen and R.J. Lange
Performed by Pedro Fernandez
Courtesy of PolyGram Discos, S.A. de C.V. - Mexico
by arrangement with PolyGram Film & TV Licensing

"I Wish You Love"
English words written by Albert Beach
French words and music written by Charles Trenet
Performed by Gloria Lynne
Courtesy of Everest Records

"Honky-Tonk Girl"
Written by H. Thompson and C. Harding
Performed by Johnny Cash
Courtesy of Columbia Records by arrangement with
Sony Music Licensing

"Your Cheatin' Heart"
Written by Hank Williams, Sr.
Performed by Patsy Cline
Courtesy of MCA Records by arrangement with
Universal Music Special Markets

"Ring of Fire"
Written by Merle Kilgore and June Carter
Performed by Johnny Cash
Courtesy of Columbia Records by arrangement with
Sony Music Licensing

"In the Upper Room With Jesus"
Written by Lucie E. Campbell
Performed by Mahalia Jackson
Courtesy of Columbia Records by arrangement with
Sony Music Licensing

"Lonesome Town"
Written by Baker Knight
Performed by Ricky Nelson
Courtesy of EMI Records under license from
EMI-Capitol Music Special Markets

"Speaking Of Happiness"
Written by Buddy Scott and Jimmy Radcliffe
Performed by Gloria Lynne
Courtesy of Black Patch Productions

"Chili Blues"
Written by Rodney Rogers and Bert Foster
Performed by R. Crumb &
The Cheap Suit Serenaders
Courtesy of Shanachie Entertainment

"Hula Girl" aka "Honolulu Hula Girl"
Written by Sunny Cunha aka Albert Sonny Cunha
Performed by R. Crumb &
The Cheap Suit Serenaders
Courtesy of Shanachie Entertainment

Lenses and Panaflex® Camera by PANAVISION®

A TRISTAR PICTURES RELEASE